zenPOWERMENT

zenPOWERMENT

*Your Path to
Peace, Power and Purpose*

RANDALL H. SCOTT

Cover designed by Mark Orton

Interior layout by Francine Eden Platt, Eden Graphics, Inc.

Randall H. Scott
Visit my site at myzenpowerment.com

Printed in the United States of America

First printing March 2018

ISBN-13: 978-1984038791

ISBN-10: 1984038796

This is for you,
That hears the whisper
and knows deep down,
there's something more,
That feels the nudge,
yet haven't moved

There is a place called home
You are already there
You just don't know it yet

TABLE OF CONTENTS

Introduction 1

Laying the Groundwork 5

    Your Hero's Journey 5

    Why I wrote this book. 7

    The Beginner's Mind 10

    Embracing Change 12

    The Slight Edge Principle. 13

    Balance and Moderation. 14

    Commitments to Yourself 15

The Zenpowerment Framework. 19

    Zenpowerment Principles 19

    How Do I Test It to See If It Works for Me? 21

    Zenpowerment Credo. 22

Understanding Authenticity 25

    Where Did Our Inauthenticity Come From? 29

    Creating Self-Awareness and Self-Examination 30

Principle 1: Living in the Present 33

    Learning and Practicing to Stay Present 36

    Being Present and Communication. 37

    Holding Space For Someone, or 'Getting' Their
    Communication 38

    Creating Perfect Present Moments 39

    Mastering Monotony 40

    Emptying the Cup / Unlearning 42

What to Keep in the Cup 45

What to Empty First From the Cup: 45

The Placebo Effect. 47

Principle 2: Standing in Your Power 49

Time and Energy, The Only True Currency,
and Our Power 49

Standing in Our Power with Our Words 56

Sameness vs. Better or Worse 57

Helping Others Stand in Their Power 58

Daily Ritual and Standing in Our Power 59

Principle 3: Coming From a Place of Love 61

The Two Great Gifts—Love and Choice. 61

Gaining a True Understanding of Unconditional
Love. 62

Balancing Love For Yourself With Love For Others. . 63

Love vs. Fear 67

How Do You Like Your Cage? 72

Accepting "What Is" as a Part of Unconditional
Love. 73

Coming From a Place of Love and Courage 75

Principle 4: The Power of Choice and Meaning 77

Power of Choice 77

The Power of Giving Meaning 79

Principle 5: Filters and Programming 81

Programming 83

Intentional Habits and Unconscious Habits 84

Programming and the Brain 85

Triggers. 88

The Path from Slavery to Mastery to Release 89

It's All Made Up. 91

Collision of Programming. 93

Choose Your Programming 94

Non-Attachment, Non-Labeling, Non-Judgment. . . . 95

Non-attachment. 95

Expectations 96

Attachment to knowledge. 97

Addiction is a form of attachment. 98

Non-labeling and Non-judgment 99

Labels divide 100

Comparison and Competition as a Form of
Judgment or Labeling. 102

Observation vs. Judgment. 102

Non-Attachment, Non-Labeling, Non-Judgment
Are Not Absolutes 102

Looking Outside of Yourself 103

Who We Really Aren't - Emotions, Feelings, Ego,
and the Body. 105

Developing Emotional Intelligence with
Zenpowerment. 106

We Are Not Our Emotions. 107

Using Emotional Triggers as Teachers 108

Developing Emotional Intelligence with Others 109

How Emotional Intelligence Gives us the Edge. 111

Emotional Bank Accounts: The Concept of the
Nickel and the Dollar. 111

Regulate the Cause, Regulate the Effect 113

Programming of Safety. 114

Knowing That You Know 115

Authority as a Filter. 115

Expectations as a Filter 116

Creating Agreement Instead of Expectations. 117

Principles vs. Rules. 117

Principle 6: Essentialism. 121

Minimalism is Just One Aspect of Essentialism 123

Being "Too Busy" 125

Smoking on It Before Buying Something. 126

The 80% / 20% Rule and Essentialism 127

The Power of Deciding 127

Principle 7: Energy and Oneness. 131

Understanding Energy 131

Energy of Resistance, Acceptance and Embracing. . 133

Maximizing our Energy. 134

Oneness 136

Brain 136

Body 137

Being. 139

Planet 139

How Things Look for You vs. How They Look
for Others. 142

Zenpowerment Tools and Habits. 143

Investing In You 143

Tools 144

Gratitude Journal 145

Meditation / Prayer / Mindfulness 146

Morning pages 148

Service 150

Exercise & Nutrition. 151

Affirmations / Visualizations:. 152

Reading 10 Pages/Day 154

Take Time to Do Nothing but Think. 155

Connect to Someone Important to You 156

Plan the Important Things in Your Day. 157

Plenty of Sleep 157

Being Okay with the Ebbs and Flows of Life. 159

The Final Chapter is Only the Beginning. 161

About the Author. 164

INTRODUCTION

As long as I can remember, I had the distinct feeling that I was going to die at age 33. I have no idea why I had this feeling, but I built my entire life around it, determined to achieve all of my goals and everything on my bucket list by that time. In my younger years, it didn't affect me as much. I was a pretty average kid, and a little rebellious as a teenager, but nothing too serious. When I turned nineteen, I served an LDS service mission in Argentina for two years, where I learned about culture, service and belief systems. At 22, I came back, got married to the woman of my dreams and started college. I only had 11 more years to live. It was time to get it all done. Within a couple of years, we had our first baby. Before I even graduated in marketing, I got a job in international sales, where I was able to earn good money and travel the world. I went skydiving, scuba diving, and sailing. I got my pilot's license and bought a small airplane. I bought the nice house and cars and everything that went along with them. I lived in Switzerland and Singapore. By the time I was 33, I had achieved almost all I had set out to do.

Then, one evening after work in the fall of 1999, I took my new motorcycle up the canyon for a quick ride before dinner. I drove up the winding road slowly, getting a feel for my new bike. It was heaven. The weather was sunny and cool. A motorcycle is best experienced on a windy canyon road, as you gently lean from side to side.

I rode to the top of the mountain pass then turned around so I could make it home in time for dinner. About halfway down the canyon, something happened and I crashed the motorcycle into the mountain on a sharp curve. To this day, I don't remember what happened that caused the crash. I thought I was gone. The first memory I had after that was waking to white light and a whirring noise. I thought, This is it. What I shortly realized was that I was in an MRI machine being examined. I was still here.

I was alive. I hadn't planned for this contingency. I no longer feared death, but what the hell was I supposed to do for the rest of my life, however long that was? You would think that I would be elated, but I struggled. I had no idea what to do with myself since I was still here. I went to a dark place. I started drinking. I got divorced. I left a job that I had been at for thirteen years. I struggled. I felt like I no longer had a purpose, or the purpose I had felt empty and meaningless.

Eventually, I realized that my entire life, I had made things happen. I was driven. I had set goals and achieved them, but my ladder was leaning against the wrong wall. I had climbed and climbed, not realizing that the destination was not really where I wanted to go. It was where society was telling me I should go. This was the beginning of my journey.

Then, I started thinking…. a lot... and studying... and

researching. I wondered what this life was really for, and if I even had any idea. I realized that what I had spent the last 33 years doing didn't really fulfill me. On the outside, it looked perfect, with the perfect wife and family, perfect job, house and amenities. So, I started my spiritual quest. I studied all kinds of spiritual practices. I had been raised Christian, and had also studied the Hindu texts. I also resonated with the Asian philosophies of Buddhism and Taoism, as well as Native American tradition. I even spent time in Peru learning from shamans. As I studied, I realized that they nearly all beliefs had a core set of common principles. These were to become staples in who I would become up to this point.

I opened myself to the Divine. Call it God, Source, or whatever you'd like, and I realized that there was a moving Force in the universe that was happy to provide assistance and direction. I realized that if I got out of my own way, and released the ego, I could accomplish much more, and make a dramatic difference in the lives of others. It was at this time that I chose to be a vessel.

The dictionary defines a vessel as an empty container, such as a glass or bowl. The value of the vessel is what it contains inside, like water or soup. The vessel is an integral part of nourishing ourselves. I realized that if I let myself be filled with the Divine, I could nourish others and be a tool for service. This is the path I chose.

I soon learned that there were things that made the vessel less effective, things like fear, attachment, judgment, and labeling. I determined the principles of love, respect, honor, trust, service were the tools that could best serve.

So, here I am today, and I've had many people ask me about my philosophy, what I believe in, and how I've come to where I am in my path. I've used this book as an outlet of my thoughts and learnings along this journey. Today, I am freer, more powerful, more authentic, and happier than I've ever been in my life. I create heaven, here and now. I am at peace. This is why I wish to share these gems.

LAYING THE GROUNDWORK

Your Hero's Journey

*I*MAGINE A LIFE of freedom and empowerment, where you can be, do and have whatever you desire. Imagine a life so powerful that you can love your enemies and face your fears, where your internal peace is the rule, and not the exception in your daily life. Imagine deep, meaningful relationships where you can be yourself, fully expressed, and be accepted for who you are. Does this sound too good to be true? It's possible.

In movies and books, there is something known as the hero's journey. In the hero's journey, there are normally three acts: departure, initiation and return. In the departure, there is the call to adventure. This is where a common person is called to do something extraordinary. Think of characters like Bilbo Baggins or Frodo in Lord of the Rings. Sometimes there is a refusal to the call, until something compels the hero to accept the call.

The initiation act is fraught with trials. This is where the hero really finds out what she/he is made of through a series of tests. This is where the lessons are learned. In many cases, he will enlist the help of others in his quest. In movies, this is where supernatural wonders show up and test the hero. This becomes the bulk of the book or movie.

The final act is the return. The return is where the hero returns triumphant, a changed person. He/she has been completely transformed by the experience.

Additionally, in most novels and movies, there is the protagonist and the antagonist, the hero and the villain. With Zenpowerment, you get to play the role of both parties. The hero is your authentic self, struggling to break free of the villain's grasp. The villain is your inauthentic self, born of fear. Or, as Steven Pressfield said in his book *Do the Work*, "On the field of the Self stand a knight and a dragon. You are the knight. Resistance is the dragon."

What if you had to give up things you always thought were true? Could you do it? What if you realized that part of your life was an illusion? How did you feel when you found out Santa Claus wasn't real? How did you shift? Would you be willing to trade what you currently believe for a new empowering reality?

What roles are you choosing to play today? Are you the victim in a relationship? Are you the dutiful employee that has squelched all his/her dreams? Are you the hero that is creating a magnificent reality for yourself?

This life is about your hero's journey. You get to choose your adventure.

What's your story? Are you ready to accept your call to adventure?

Why I wrote this book

What if you knew that in a week or a month, you were going to die? How would that affect every single thing you do? How would it change your interactions with people? How much would you worry about things that don't really matter? What would you do differently?

Every day, we are one day closer to death. We may not know exactly when that day will come, which is even more reason to live each moment fully and deeply, without regrets. When I thought that I was going to die at age 33, I planned for it. I embraced it, and that made all the difference. When we no longer fear something, it loses its power over us.

When we get comfortable with the fact that we are all on our way to dying, it becomes liberating. When we no longer fear death, we can truly live. Change this one perspective in your life, and you can change everything.

I wrote this book with the intent to blow your mind, and to shift your perspective. It may be a single concept or phrase, or a bunch of this content may create that change, but I want to blow your mind and create a new possibility for your life. Manal Maurice put it this way:

> "Breakthroughs happen not because of startling new facts, but because of a change in the overall way that the universe is seen. Nothing is more exciting than to see the world in a new way, because we don't see one new thing—we see everything in a new way."

I have applied these principles in varying degrees over the past eighteen years and have found incredible freedom, joy, and peace. I want to create clear, concise, and compelling content that makes your journey into authenticity easier and flowing.

Have you ever asked yourself:

- Why does life seem so easy for other people, but difficult for me?

- What is my purpose?

- Why do I have such a great life, but am still unhappy?

- Why am I so afraid of what other people think?

- Why does it feel like I attract drama into my life?

These are questions that many people deal with, or have dealt with, along their journey of life.

We are all like computers or mobile phones—we all have programming. Just like computers and mobile phones have an operating system, we have been programmed with an operating system. We have been programmed by our parents, schooling, society, marketing, nation, corporations, government, and other influences. Think about these questions and ask yourself if you do these things, and why you do them:

- Do I buy gifts or do something special for my parents or significant other on a day that was specified by the government (Mother's day, Father's Day, Valentine's Day)?

- Do we live by the clock, hour by hour, day by day? How did people get by before time was 'invented'? Do I live based on the planets, rising & setting of sun, moon/month, January after Janus the Roman God, 7 days in a week because there are 7 visible planets?

- Do we buy into an education and corporate work system that was created during the industrial revolution of replaceable parts and people, where it was necessary to conform and be a cog in a manufacturing assembly line? Does that still serve us today?

- Do we live in fear of what others will think of us? Are we looking for approval and acceptance outside of ourselves?

- Do we accept what corporate, government, and religious leaders tell us, just because of who they are? Do we question authority? For example, if we are told by someone in authority to do something or believe something, do we still question it, to make sure it aligns with our values and beliefs?

- Do we just accept learned behavior such as racism, sexism, and other forms of bigotry?

- Do we apply labels and judgments that our parents and friends taught us? Just because our parents or friends believed something, is it really true, or have we just accepted their belief system as our own?

When we realize that we have all been programmed, then we can do something about it. When we create awareness of how much of our lives is reactive, pre-conditioned response, then we can make a change. There is nothing inherently wrong with these things. Some of our programming is very beneficial, but when we open our awareness that there may be another way, we open up new possibilities.

The Beginner's Mind

Confirmation bias is defined as the tendency to interpret new evidence as confirmation of one's existing beliefs or theories. This means that when we take on new information, we give it meaning based on what we already believe. Not only that, we actively search out information that supports our point of view. An example of confirmation bias is when you buy a car. As soon as you buy a car, you start seeing the same type of car all over the place. This helps support your decision that you made a good choice. This is a filter that our brain has created to make us more efficient. Unfortunately, it is not always most beneficial. It can limit our learning and growth. The tighter we hold onto our existing beliefs, the less we can learn new things.

Another element that we encounter as we learn new things is cognitive dissonance. Cognitive dissonance is defined as the state of having inconsistent thoughts, beliefs, or attitudes, especially as relating to behavioral decisions and attitude change. This means that we have two pieces of information that contradict each other and we look to determine how to rationalize them in our brain. This can be a cause of stress until we resolve this through accepting one idea and rejecting the other, or by rationalizing in our minds how we can accept both ideas.

When I lived in Argentina, I was invited to dinner at a very poor home. They had saved money just so they could provide me with the meal. As they poured the milk into my cup, I saw large curdles of milk plopping into the cup. As I was eating the bread, I noticed these huge pieces of fat in the bread. The meal was horrible, but I knew the sacrifice that this lady had made so that I could share a meal with her. I believe that lying is bad, but I also believe that hurting somebody's feelings, especially after so much sacrifice, is also bad. When she asked me how the food was, I chose to lie, and say that it was a great meal. I felt that lying to her was less harmful than hurting her feelings.

As you read this book, there may be information that doesn't align with your current belief system. In fact, it might be in direct opposition to what you currently believe. You may feel angry, confused or want to discard the information because of your discomfort. Don't discard the information immediately. You may just be hitting against some filters and programming that you already have in place.

There is a Buddhist concept called shoshin, or the beginner's mind. In shoshin, the idea is to set aside all knowledge and beliefs that you currently have while you are learning something new. You start with a clean slate so that you don't filter out anything inadvertently through confirmation bias or any other filters that you may have. By doing this, the amount of true learning becomes exponential. In the end, you don't have to accept everything you learn, but you are more open to see things from a different perspective. You may apply your filters afterward if it is beneficial.

Whenever I give a presentation or start a coaching engagement, I ask the people or person to approach our conversation with the beginner's mind. I even tell them that I may be wrong, but that the principles work for me.

I would ask that you practice shoshin as you read

this book. Some aspects may serve, some may not, but the concepts in this book will provide greater value if you approach them with the beginner's mind. Whenever I approach a topic with the curiosity of a child, I get much more out of it than if I think I know everything.

Embracing Change

This book is about change. If you embrace these principles, you will change. We, as humans, are programmed to resist change. What's interesting is, nothing is permanent. Everything changes, so when we resist change, we are fighting reality.

Embrace change. Sometimes it will be exhilarating. Sometimes painful. But always worth it.

You get to do the work. You don't just read this book and put it down and become a more authentic you. The miracle is in the practice. Knowledge is learning; wisdom is application. I've been doing this for eighteen years now, and I still feel like a baby. I still get caught up in my limiting beliefs and get to change and let them go. I am, however, more authentic than I've ever been, and I love the fact that there is never an 'arriving.' There is always room to grow and learn.

Other people in your life will recognize this. Some will be accepting of your change, some will not. Like the story of the crabs in the pan, you will be getting yourself out of the pan, and others around you will try to pull you down. As you see and feel this, just be aware of it. Some friends may fall away from your life, while new friends enter. This is normal, expected, and welcomed. Even you may try to sabotage yourself, because you resist the changes that you are creating within yourself. At the same time, you will be changing, so you will start to see others differently than you have. At times, you will think that it's them changing, when really it's you changing, so your perspective of them changes.

Change causes uncertainty. Uncertainty causes fear. We must face the fear with love. None of us can control the future, but we can control our reaction to it. We can control our thoughts about it. Since we can control our response, and we get to choose love over fear, we will always get a better response by proactively choosing to act instead of react, and to come from a place of love. This concept may seem vague now, but we will get into a lot of detail about love versus fear later on in the book.

This is easier said than done. It takes continual practice. It can be challenging facing and changing a lifetime of programming, filters, and habits. Believe it or not, there may actually be a benefit or payoff that we receive for continuing with these unhealthy programs. There are, however, costs as well. My experience has been that when I have implemented these principles, and been diligent, my life, my freedom, and my power have been much greater.

The Slight Edge Principle

In his book *The Slight Edge*, Jeff Olson describes how small, incremental habits, done over time, have a compounding effect, for either good or bad. We create our lives on a grand scale by the small, repeatable decisions and habits that we make. The interesting thing about these small habits is that they are easy to do, and at the same time, easy not to do. The magic occurs in the compounding effect over time.

For example, if you were to put $10,000 in an investment making interest, and you looked at it every day or every week, you wouldn't see much difference. If you looked at it five or ten years later, you'd be more impressed. It's the same thing with creating a daily ritual. If you go to the gym for an hour a day for a week, you're not going to notice huge changes. Over time, it will pay off.

Throughout the journey of this book, I will recommend tools and habits that can assist with implementing and integrating these principles in your life. They are an investment in you. Choose those tools and habits that serve you, and commit to them. Each of these tools and habits has power on their own, but together, their power is synergistic, and the sum is greater than the individual parts. Additionally, over time, these habits build residual benefits.

Balance and Moderation

The underlying theme of many of these principles is balance and moderation. If we have a balance in self-love and love for others, we don't become a narcissist or a martyr. If we create an exercise and diet program, we can take care of this temporary vessel so that it serves us well. We can also take these principles too far, be too extreme, which turns us into the servants of these principles, instead of their master.

Just like water, a drink of water can replenish us, but a

flood of water can drown us. As you evaluate these principles, try them on and see if they serve. Some will serve you more than others. Some will serve you for a period of time until they no longer benefit you. Use them as guidelines to uncover who you are.

There is also a compounding effect as you create a balance between physical, mental, spiritual, and emotional investment in yourself. There is spillover between these aspects of ourselves. For example, if you exercise, you will also feel more mental clarity. Also, over time, each of these small investments will provide huge dividends.

Commitments to Yourself

Whenever I start a coaching engagement with a new client, I ask them to commit to four things:

1. **Make a commitment, keep a commitment** – Commitments allow us to create new habits. They get us uncomfortable until they become comfortable. They help us grow. As you go through this book, I will recommend tools and habits for your benefit. The more you commit to, the greater the growth.

   If you make a commitment and break it, don't beat up yourself. Commitment is a muscle that needs to be exercised. It will grow stronger over time. Measure yourself against progress, not perfection.

2. **Journal the journey** – In Julia Cameron's book *The Artist's Way*, she describes a practice called morning pages. The concept of morning pages is to write

three pages every day. Write about anything you want, but write. Free flow writing is what may benefit you most.

We have all been programmed in our writing. As we learned to write in school, we self-edited in the process. We wrote, thinking about what would get us the best grade from the teacher. I wrote in a personal journal for many years, but I always edited as well, thinking, "do I want my posterity to know about this?" With morning pages, they should be completely unedited. This is a great place to get out all your emotions, to work through things that are on your mind, and to expand your creativity. If you are angry at your spouse, and want to call them a million swear words, do it in your morning pages. If you want to throw your kids at the wall for how they are behaving, do it in your morning pages. Create a habit and a safe space where you can actually experience all of your thoughts and emotions. This is also a place where you can decide what to do with them in the real world, and what will serve you best.

I do my morning pages on my computer, in a password protected document. Some prefer to do them with pen and paper. At first, morning pages seem tedious and not beneficial, because you are learning a new habit and breaking old ones. As you stick to them, they become incredibly valuable. This is a safe place to work through emotions that wouldn't serve in a conversation with others. This is where your creativity can play. There are many times when I am inspired during my writing and come up with a great idea or a great blog post. I simply copy those things that I want to share and put them in another place.

I have also found that doing my morning pages right after meditation allows for greater intuition and inspiration. During meditation, I am able to increase alpha brain waves, which contribute to creativity.

A buddy of mine paraphrased a quote that goes something like this, *"You don't know what you think until you hear what you say or read what you wrote."* I have seen this time and time again in my morning pages. It provides clarity and insight that I cannot get in any other way.

Throughout this book, I will recommend morning page exercises that will allow you be introspective and go deeper into your own internal world. These may feel uncomfortable, and you may feel resistance to doing them because you may have to give up a part of who you think you are. This is part of the authentic journey. I request that you do the work and free yourself.

3. **Share the nuggets** – There are two benefits in sharing the concepts that you find valuable in this book. First, as you teach somebody else what you've learned, you integrate it more fully into your life. You add your perspective on it. Second, if it's something that helps you, perhaps it will help another. This is a great way to pay it forward.

4. **Be honest with yourself** – During the process of uncovering your authenticity, you will encounter resistance, change, and discomfort. Sometimes, you will know why. Other times, there will be things in your subconscious that will cause resistance, and you won't even realize it. Additionally, as humans, we tend to cover up our dark sides and things we're not proud of. We put them away in a dusty corner in the basement of our minds. Use this book and process to look at all of you. We all have our shit. Don't hide it from yourself. Be brutally honest and vulnerable, especially in your morning pages. With time, you will see the benefits in embracing all of who you are.

Even though this is not a personal engagement between you and me, I still request that you make these commitments to yourself. It is only for your benefit.

THE ZENPOWERMENT
FRAMEWORK

Zenpowerment Principles

THERE ARE A NUMBER OF PRINCIPLES that create a sense of power and perspective along life's journey. These are things that I have found to be a foundation for getting to really know who I am, making the most of my life, and continuously improving myself. Principles are the things that are steadfast, immovable, and can be counted on. They don't change with time. I use these as anchors. We will delve into each one of these principles and habits, but for the sake of a top-level overview, here are the seven key principles that will be covered:

- Living in the present
- Standing in your power
- Coming from a place of love
- The power of choice and meaning
- Understanding and eliminating filters and programming

- Essentialism and minimalism

- Energy and oneness

What I've learned about applying these principles and habits in my life is that they are all intertwined. Each one helps the other. Sometimes one of the principles shows up needing more attention, so I focus on it more strongly for a time. Sometimes, one or more of the principles becomes dominant during an activity, a decision, or for a season. By applying all of these principles, at whatever depth possible, a continual happiness and improvement in quality of life will occur.

We create the quality of our lives through every choice we make based on the thoughts we have, the principles we hold true, and the habits we've created. Zenpowerment is the process of creating empowerment through changing your perspective through the principles and habits of Zen. In this book, Zen is very loosely interpreted as a philosophy and number of principles that have helped me along my journey. It gets its roots from many forms of spirituality and religion, including Buddhism, Hinduism, Taoism, Christianity, and Native American teachings. It is very experiential in nature, focusing on the journey and not the goal.

Zenpowerment has completely changed my life, and continues to do so. My request to you, dear reader, is to try on these principles. Test them, see if they resonate. If they do, great. If they don't, great. Zenpowerment has created miracles in my life for the past eighteen years, but tomorrow, they may no longer serve me, and I'll release them. Give them a try and see what they do for you.

How Do I Test It to See If It Works for Me?

This is the fun part, and the difficult part. I'm going to share a number of principles and habits with you. You get to try them on, see if they work, and accept or reject them as you wish.

Think about it. *We do things consciously and unconsciously. If we can bring the things that we do unconsciously into our conscious, to evaluate them and accept or reject them, then we can act out of place of conscious intent.* When we create a new way of thinking, we create a new construct, a new way of seeing things. We can then test this new construct to see how it affects our perspective on everything and on life. Part of this includes removing any blocks or filters on the way we see things.

For example, a common fear that we hold is the fear of what other people think about us. Most of the time this is an unconscious habit. We choose not to speak up or act because of our fear of what others think of us. We continually look for external validation from others. When we become aware of how much we do this, we can start to evaluate when it is more beneficial for us to speak up or act, regardless of the fear programming that we have been running. After a while of practicing this, it becomes a new habit, and we become much more self-expressed because we no longer fear what others think about us.

If the principle benefits your life, keep with it. If it doesn't, feel free to discard it for now. Later on, you might want to pick it back up and integrate it into your life. As I have coached these principles, I have seen that some principles resonate more with some people than with others.

I have also learned that concepts that I had minimally focused on were universally important to every client, so I included more detail on those items in this book.

It seems like the learning of each of these principles is never-ending. By applying them intentionally in my life, I seem to go deeper down the rabbit hole in the breadth and depth of each principle. One example that has been extremely profound is the principle of non-attachment. I thought I had a good understanding of non-attachment years ago, but as I continue to apply it in my life, I continue to see other ways in which attachment causes suffering, as the Buddha said.

Zenpowerment Credo

A credo is a statement of beliefs that guides our actions. In a sense, it is an affirmation of who we choose to be and how we choose to act—like a simple blueprint for our life. As I was coaching executives while writing this book, one of them suggested that I create a summary of Zenpowerment that they could refer back to from time to time. While this may not all make sense now, I wanted to present it here as a summary. Once you've gone through the principles in this book, it will make much more sense to you. This is my credo:

Zenpowerment Credo

1. There are two primary motivational forces in our lives; love and fear. Love unites, fear divides. Love accepts, fear resists. Love is proactive, fear

is reactive. Love is intrinsic, fear is learned. With love, there must be a balance between love for ourselves and love for others. This balance is created by boundaries. **I choose love.**

2. I give away my power when I come from fear or choose to react from programming. **I choose to stand in my power.**

3. I am responsible for all that is in my life. I have the power to choose my response and to give meaning to all circumstances. **I choose to stand in my power.**

4. I cannot change the past. It has been a great teacher, and I honor it. My future is not guaranteed, but I can establish a direction for my future. The only thing that really exists is here and now. It is the only place of power and action. **I choose to live intentionally in the present.**

5. My authenticity has been covered by years of filters and programming, through family, education, corporations, culture, government, tradition, authority, and many other things. Filters and programming include attachment, judgments, labels, expectations, comparison, emotions, and our experiences. I empty my cup of knowledge to see what still serves and what does not. I choose to always keep the principles of love, trust, respect, communication, service, gratitude, and fun in my cup. **I choose to uncover my authenticity**.

6. I believe that attachment to opinions, knowledge, people, things, expectations, outcomes, thoughts, emotions, the past, and future causes great suffering. **I choose non-attachment**.

7. I believe that saying no to the many unessential things allows me greater time and energy to focus on those things I deem important. By doing this, I become more efficient. **I choose to live essentially**.

8. I have believed that I am a separate, independent being. I now believe that we are all interconnected beings, all made up of energy. **I choose love for all living things**.

9. Every act and habit empowers or disempowers me, and continues to build up over time. I am a sum of my thoughts, words, actions, and habits. **I choose empowering habits.**

10. **I choose empowerment by living intentionally and authentically.**

Once you've had a chance to read this book and implement those things that resonate with you, create your own credo that represents what you stand for.

UNDERSTANDING AUTHENTICITY

"If everyone were cast in the same mold, there would be no such thing as beauty."

– CHARLES DARWIN

"To express our individuality is to reclaim our divinity."

– DEBBIE FORD

DO YOU REALLY KNOW who you are? Do you know who you're not? Maybe, just maybe, if you can figure out who you are not, you can get closer to figuring out who you are. Perhaps, if you crumble away those things that you know are definitely not you, you can find the essence of who you truly are. As you think about these questions, ask yourself if these things are NOT who you really are:

- Am I my material possessions? Am I my car or the size of my home? Am I my debt and unpaid bills?
- Am I who I am based on the opinions of others?
- Am I my job or social status? Am I my lack of job?

- Am I the filters that have been created through my upbringing, my social status, my sex, my race, my authority figures, etc.?

- Am I my thoughts?

- Am I my emotions and feelings?

- Am I my body? Do I get my identity from my workout schedule or what I look like?

- Am I the stories I've created about myself (not being good enough, not being loved, being abandoned, etc.)

- Am I the self-judgments I make on myself every day?

If you can answer *no* to these questions, then perhaps you may be closer to knowing who you authentically are. Or, as you're reading this, you're using the filters, thoughts and emotions to justify where you are. In any case, it's food for thought.

What does authenticity mean to you? How would you define it? Do you believe that people that are closest to you are authentic? Are you?

Most of us believe that we are authentic, but what if we're really not? What if there were more? What if we could redefine authenticity so that we could live a life with more freedom, abundance and self-expression than we ever thought possible? What if we could define our authenticity as we wish?

Ask yourself these questions:

- Do I act or not act out of fear of what others might think of me?

- How often do I act without thinking, like I'm on autopilot, just because it's what I've always done?

- Are my thoughts, feelings, words, and actions in alignment?

- How do I act when nobody is watching?

- Do I not speak up when I believe differently, just to keep the peace?

- Do I accept my dark side as well as my light side?

Most of us really try to do our best at being authentic, however not being aware of some of the causes of inauthenticity create blind spots in ourselves. A blind spot is something that is not in our conscious, or that we're not aware of. Our blind spots may be visible by other people, but completely hidden from us. They are the things that we do not know that we do not know.

Authenticity is an interesting characteristic. One definition from the Merriam-Webster dictionary is:

true to one's own personality, spirit, or character.

In other words, it is being true to yourself. It is not acting out of fear of what other people think. It is not acting out of programming that you accepted as truth. An important aspect of authenticity is integrity, when what you think, feel, say, and do are in alignment (a quote from Ghandi). It is knowing that when you give your word, It doesn't matter if you're giving it to the CEO or to the garbage person, it's about who you are, not who they are. It's about being wise in making commitments, so you know you'll be able to keep them.

Another aspect of integrity is self-betrayal. Self-betrayal occurs when we fail to listen to our intuition because we talk ourselves out of it. When we betray ourselves, we start to see the world in a way that justifies our behavior. Our view of reality becomes distorted. When we betray others, we inflate the faults of others and minimize our own, to inflate our virtues.

Authenticity is the practice of standing in our power. It is the essence of who we choose to be when we act intentionally. It is what remains when unhealthy programming and filters have been removed, or at least evaluated and consciously chosen. It's like when Michelangelo sculpted the David statue from a huge piece of marble, and removed everything that wasn't David. It's shattering away the illusions, disintegrating untruth, and seeing what's left. It's the crumbling of one reality so that a new reality may be seen.

This is how Adyashanti describes enlightenment, but it resonates with authenticity as well:

> *"Make no mistake about it—enlightenment is a destructive process. It has nothing to do with becoming better or being happier. Enlightenment is the crumbling away of untruth. It's seeing through the facade of pretense. It's the complete eradication of everything we imagined to be true."*

As you go deeper into your authentic self, and peel away the layers, you will be shaken over and over again. There will be a cycle of questioning, of fearing "what happens if I let go of what I've known to be true?", of reestablishing self on a new foundation, and then an increased feeling of liberation, empowerment, and peace. Each aspect of yourself that you choose to inspect will go through this cycle, but you will know that you will come through the other side in a more empowering state of being. As you go through this process, just remember, you have made it through 100% of the challenges you've had in your life. Those are pretty good odds.

My background is in marketing. When I engage with a company, one of the first things that we do is craft their unique value proposition. This is what sets them apart from the competition. It is what makes them special. It is why customers buy from them. Our authenticity is our unique value proposition as a human being. What sets you apart? What are you remembered for?

Where Did Our Inauthenticity Come From?

We don't wake up every day and say to ourselves, "How can I be inauthentic?" Most of us just don't realize where and why we have become this way. We learned to be inauthentic.

When we were born, we were this amazing, beautiful clean slate of love and joy. We were authenticity at its best. We were dependent on others to live (and to not stink when our diapers needed changing). When we were hungry, tired, or sleepy, we had one response; cry. With time, we learned that crying got the attention of our caretakers, and would make everything alright.

As we started to grow, we were learning sponges. Whatever anyone told us, we just believed. Our favorite word was *why*. Somewhere along the way, our learning and our brains introduced us to the concepts of fear and shame. These things didn't feel so good, so we figured out ways to avoid them or hide from them. Just like a crab, we created these 'shells' to protect our soft insides and feelings. The more difficult the circumstances, the thicker the shell.

As we continued to grow, we wanted happiness and fulfillment. We looked to others to see what they were doing. Some people focused on their bodies, some on their jobs, some on their friends and family, some on their belonging, and a bunch of other things. We started to emulate those things to find our own happiness. If everybody else is doing it, it must be right. Right?

After a while, we became like robots, and accepted the life we lived as our reality. Yet, somewhere deep inside, we realized that something was missing. There was something more.

Creating Self-Awareness and Self-Examination

We uncover our authenticity through awareness. Awareness is created by being present and mindful. Our experience is made up of subject and objects. Your authentic self is the subject, the witness to all that is happening. Everything else is objects. Your thoughts, feelings, and experiences are all objects that your authentic self witnesses. The problem is that, most of the time we think these objects are us, or our authentic self. We collapse our thoughts and emotions on top of who we really are. These things are not us. They are things we have or experience.

One of the key things to uncover your authenticity is to create habits of self-awareness and self-examination. This can be done most effectively through meditation and mindfulness, to be discussed in detail later in this book. Another key tool is morning pages, where you can contemplate and evaluate why you do what you do. By being present, you can determine if you are being intentional, or if you are reacting with programming. As you evaluate your life and your motives, see if you can identify any places where you are being inauthentic. See if there are times when you act out of fear of what others might think of you. The more you become aware of your motives, the more you can chisel away those actions that are not the authentic you.

By creating awareness of your actions and motives, you begin to live an intentional life. Awareness also forces you to be in the here and now, instead of thinking about the past or worrying about the future. Here and now is all there really is.

At first, when you begin to live from a place of awareness, you'll most likely recognize programming and inauthenticity after it shows up. That's okay. Becoming authentic and empowered is a process. It will take time to be able to recognize it before you react, but with practice, you will become more intentional and authentic.

PRINCIPLE 1

LIVING IN THE PRESENT

"There are only two days in which you have no control or can do nothing about. One is yesterday, the other is tomorrow."

—DALAI LAMA

*H*OW MUCH TIME do you spend thinking about that one mistake you made, or that one regret you have? How much time do you relive the divorce you went through, the argument with your son, that time you got fired? How much time do you spend relishing the good ol' days? How much time do you spend having that conversation in your head with somebody that never happens? How much time do you worry about your future, and *what happens if this goes wrong?*

Many people suffer from "destination addiction." They decide that they will find happiness when A, B, or C occurs, whatever that next destination is. Unfortunately, **if you can't be happy here and now, you'll never be happy there and then.**

What if, all of a sudden, you had amnesia and couldn't remember a thing? How would that change your life? Now think about all of your past. How many of your present moments are being burdened because you live in the past? How many times do you relive those *bad* decisions you made? When you're looking to achieve a new goal, how many times do you bring yourself down because you're comparing who you are today to who you were five or ten years ago?

Time is an illusion which we are forced to experience on this planet. In all actuality, all we can really experience is the present moment. If we had no memory, we could not experience time. Time is fabricated by our memory connecting all of our present moments. We can remember the past, and we can hope for the future, but the only thing we can directly affect is the here and now. Here and now is the only point of action. You can't change the past, and the only thing you can do about the future is what you do now. For this reason, my goal at all times is to create as many perfect present moments as possible. If we do so, then we can look back on our lives and see a multitude of perfect present moments connected together to make an amazing life up to the present moment.

> *"Make your plans in pencil, live in the present, and let the Divine guide you along the way."* –RANDY SCOTT

Living in the present takes practice. It takes awareness and mastery of our thoughts. It takes learning to be present and practicing mindfulness. There are times, however, when thinking about the future or past are beneficial. Examples of beneficial future contemplation include:

- Establishing and reviewing goals (made in pencil, of course!)

- Planning my day and calendaring events
- Mentally preparing for important conversations or presentations that are really going to happen
- Planning vacations
- Creating business plans and strategy

Beneficial past reflection includes:

- Lessons learned that can be presently applied
- Identifying my stories and programming of the past that are affecting my present life
- Memories of family, friends, etc., without over-thinking

It is enjoyable to reminisce about the past and dream about the future. There is value in learning from the lessons of the past, as well as creating plans for the future. The danger, however, is when we spend too much time in the past or future. If we relive mistakes over and over that we made in the past, or dwell on that *perfect* relationship we had and lost, we lose valuable present moments that could be used otherwise. Conversely, when we look to the future, thinking, "*I'll be happy when….*" or, "*Life will be much better when….*", we also lose the opportunity to create happiness here and now, or take action towards those future plans.

For each moment that we spend thinking about the future or the past, we give up the opportunity to create a perfect present moment. It's a decision on how we choose to use our time and energy.

When we learn to stay present, we are able to create awareness. Awareness is the key to evaluating and eliminating programming that no longer serves us. It allows us to extend that sacred space between stimulus and response, so that we can learn to respond instead of react. Being present also allows us to enjoy that specific time in life more deeply. When we choose to stay in the here and now, we intentionally choose the life we want to live, instead of letting our programming run our lives.

Since now is the only point of action, the more we learn to stay present, the more time and energy we have to dedicate to whatever it is we choose to achieve. Instead of worrying about the past which we cannot change, or thinking about doing something in the future, we can do it right now. When we couple living in the present with the principle of essentialism, then we know we are focusing on the right things for us, and we're taking action to get things done more efficiently.

Learning and Practicing to Stay Present

Staying present isn't always easy, especially at first, because we haven't disciplined our minds from wandering. Most of us spend an inordinate amount of time thinking about our past, about what we enjoyed, about what we could have done better. Many times, we live in regret or shame about decisions we made. I have one piece of advice.... STOP IT! The past has passed. There is nothing you can do about it, and the more time you spend pondering on the past, the more present time you are wasting. Learn from the past, but stay present. If you don't stay present, you'll recreate your past, simply based on your programming.

Many of us choose to live in the future, making plans, hoping that once X or Y happens, we will finally be happy. Again, I implore... STOP IT! Be happy now. Don't wait for some event to create happiness. Be happy now. One of the best pieces of advice I can give regarding the future is, "Make your plans in pencil, be present, and let the Divine nudge you along the way." This has created the most impactful, happy life I could have imagined. Sure, I create direction in my life through planning for the future, but when it doesn't happen exactly as I plan, I'm okay with that. I know that the Divine has a better plan for me that I couldn't see at the time. I direct my life with my intention, then surrender to the ebbs and flows of life. Looking back, it's easy to see how my life continues to turn out better than I could have imagined when I follow this guideline.

Being Present and Communication

Being present during communication is not only a great way to practice being present, but it will create miracles in your communication. Think about it. How many times are you in a conversation, and before the other person is even done speaking, you are preparing your reply? This is so common, especially in the Western world.

Practice staying present in a conversation. When somebody is speaking, do nothing but listen intently to them. When they are done speaking, take time to think about what they said, and about your response. As you think about your response, take care not to reply just to defend your opinion or ego. Really receive what they have to say.

Value what they have to say. Try to understand what they have to say.

Holding Space For Someone, or 'Getting' Their Communication

Holding space for someone, or 'getting' somebody's communication is key in creating a communication bridge. Getting somebody's communication means really being present until the end, being empathetic to their position, and letting them know that you get how they feel. You don't have to agree with somebody to understand how they feel. You don't have to attach to your opinion of what you think is the truth or right, to know how they feel. You just need to listen and understand their position. Consider an opinion as just an interesting point of view. When you learn to get somebody else's communication, you move forward in your skills as a communicator.

Good communication occurs when you're exchanging information with the intent of a better understanding of a situation. When one person starts to get defensive or tries to defend their own opinion, then the communication stops. When the ego gets involved, then you are trying to defend who is right, instead of what is right. At this time, it is better to stop the conversation, and wait until later, when both parties can be more objective, and really try to understand the other person's point of view. It is important to identify the times when someone wants two-way communication versus just wanting to express themselves. If they just want to express themselves, holding space for them is the greatest gift you can give.

Creating Perfect Present Moments

If the only point of action is the present moment, then creating as many perfect present moments as possible is a worthwhile endeavor. Just being present helps increase the quality and quantity of perfect present moments.

Mindfulness is the Buddhist concept of light meditation. It is being fully present, without judgment. It is noticing your thoughts and emotions without attaching to them. For example, when you sit down for a meal, completely experience the food. Be present. Taste the flavor, temperature, and texture of each bite. Consider how it feels to chew each bite. When you swallow, sense how it travels down your esophagus. Experience the meal as if it were your first time eating.

One way I like to take this experience a step further is to practice grateful mindfulness. In the example above of eating, I look at the whole ecosphere of my eating experience. I'm grateful for all of the people that participated in bringing the meal to my table. The farmers that grew the food, the animal that gave its life for me to integrate its energy into mine. The soil, water, and sunshine that allowed the food to grow. The truck driver that delivered it to my market. When we practice grateful mindfulness, it gives us a whole new perspective of appreciation for how interconnected we all are.

Another aspect of mindfulness is to practice everything. Perfect each experience as it comes up, whether it be playing an instrument or doing the dishes. As we learn to remain present, practice mindfulness, and make each moment a continual practice of improvement, we will create more and more perfect present moments.

There are no little things. There are no inconsequential moments. Everything that is present matters... and it doesn't. It's whatever you choose. Just be present for them.

Mastering Monotony

Monotony is defined as "lack of variety and interest; tedious repetition and routine." There are many things we do on a daily basis that become habit, and sometimes even monotonous. There are some things that we have to do that we don't even like doing. In our work and home routines, some things just have to get done. Additionally, there are things that we really want to conquer in life, yet they also get old and tiring. According to Malcolm Gladwell's *Outliers*, becoming an expert takes doing something 10,000 times. So, as we're becoming experts, how do we overcome monotony?

Here are a few suggestions:

1. **Live fully in the present** – At times, monotony increases when we're doing something and thinking of 100 other things that we'd rather be doing. For me, this happens with activities such as doing dishes, showering, driving, and making my bed. If we pay attention to the task at hand, not only do we do it better, the monotony of the activity decreases, and we possibly get it done faster.

2. **Improve/perfect the mundane** – I was invited to a Japanese tea ceremony (an example can be found

at www.youtube.com/watch?v=7tt7NBIVeMY) when I was in Japan. At first I thought *boring*, but decided to be a good visitor and experience the local culture. I make tea all the time, and it's not that difficult. What I witnessed was a beautiful exhibition of perfection, culture, and pride in making and serving tea. There was precision and care taken in the preparation of the dry tea, the placement of the cups, cleansing of the vessels, and the pouring of the water. It became artistic.

As we perform mundane tasks, we should ask ourselves how we can improve or perfect whatever we're doing. We may not want to become an *expert* in brushing teeth, washing our truck, or washing dishes, but we might learn to enjoy them more, and do them better.

3. **Look through 'new eyes'** – When one of my kids was four years old, the bathtub overflowed, leaving about a 1/2 inch of water on the floor. I started grabbing towels, buckets, and anything I could find to quickly clean up the mess. I asked my son to find something to help. He brought a dust pan. It was perfect for the task at hand, but I hadn't even thought of it.

    In the movie *Dead Poets Society* with Robin Williams, Robin (the teacher) asked the students to stand on their desks to gain a new perspective. Many times, if we look at the same activity with 'new eyes,' we may find a new way to do it more efficiently, or we may find a new way to enjoy it.

It's been said that anything worth doing is worth doing well. It's also been been said that the little things ARE the big things. As we learn to overcome monotony, improve the mundane, and live fully in the present, the monotonous can become miraculous.

When we choose to master monotonous tasks, we can improve them. There are, however, benefits with just letting our autopilot take care of the monotonous tasks, so that we can use our conscious thought to focus on other things. The good thing is that each of us can consciously choose how to use our time and energy during these tasks.

Emptying the Cup / Unlearning

"All you have to do is let go of who you think you are. That's it—plain and simple. Cast away all those useless dramas and become nothing, an eternal zero, an emptiness that is abundantly full and wisely alert." – ADYASHANTI

Since we as humans are constantly evolving, we are constantly learning. An important aspect of evolution is unlearning things that are not true or no longer serve us. The less we think we know, the more open we can be to new learning. If we believe we know everything (cup is full), we don't allow much space for new learning. In our lives, there should be a constant process of learning, unlearning, and relearning.

Much of the learning that doesn't serve us is from our childhood, when our decision-making ability was not yet honed. Many things we considered traumatic as a child would not phase us today, but the programming of our childhood is already imprinted in our minds, and continues to run, even though we may not even be aware. For example, we may have been the last one picked for kickball in the second grade, and we created the program that we are unwanted or not good enough. Once this program was established, we looked for evidence to support this program (confirmation bias). Since we were looking, we found it, time and time again, so it supported the program. Now, here we are today, and we're still running the same program, and it doesn't serve.

How do we find this unwanted programming if it is running in our subconscious? How do we identify it if we're not even aware of it? One way is our reactions. If something triggers us or creates an unusually high emotional response based on the circumstance, there's a good chance that there is some programming that no longer serves. Whenever we are triggered, it is good to remember that it has nothing to do with the other person. They didn't do it to us. They simply showed us an area within ourselves that we can work on. Triggers are gifts. They are our teachers.

Another way to find unwanted programming is to identify patterns in your life that are not serving you. Do you continually attract the same type of unhealthy relationships into your life? Do you continually have a lack of money? Do you use addiction to escape from the reality of your life? These things are pointing to something deeper in your unconscious programming that no longer serve you, where you would benefit from unlearning and releasing that programming.

The analogy of emptying the cup has served me well.

If a cup is full, you can no longer put anything else in it. If the cup is mostly empty, it can be filled as desired.

The more we strip away stories, programming, and filters in our lives, the more open we become to inspiration. There is a saying that success is 1% inspiration and 99% perspiration. In a life of Zenpowerment, inspiration is a much higher number, and the perspiration is much less, as ease and flow are a big part of how life shows up.

It's amazing to realize how many things we believe are true or real, and really aren't. They are stories that we have created, so they create our reality. It's also interesting to see how many things we've learned and still hold onto, even though they no longer serve.

A key ingredient of emptying the cup is not being attached to what is in the cup. The stronger we attach to what we believe, the more difficult it is to let it go. Our knowledge can become an addiction.

Nature abhors a vacuum. When an empty space is created, the universe will fill it. This is a law in physics. The same law applies in our lives. When we create an empty space in our time, material possessions, or the people in our lives, these empty spaces will get filled. If we are looking to always improve ourselves, then we should let go of things with lower vibrations, so it can be replaced with things of higher vibration. This is one of the principles behind emptying the cup. We want to always create a vacuum so that we have a place to be filled with new learning, insight and inspiration.

Where do you choose to create a vacuum in your life? What do you choose to fill it with?

What to Keep in the Cup

Do you guide your life by principles or by rules, or by nothing at all? What is the compass of your soul? What gives you direction?

An important distinction that I like to make is the difference between a principle and a rule. For me, principles are everlasting. They are beliefs that are consistent universally when they are applied. Most rules are made up by men, and are not universal. They work in some situations and not it others. They are adopted by some cultures, but not others.

In the bottom of my cup, I keep principles that always serve me. They are love, honor, trust, respect, service, and gratitude. These have always served me, and I believe they always will. My understanding of these principles has grown and developed over the years as I've applied them in my life, but I choose to keep these principles in the bottom of my cup.

You get to choose what to keep in your cup and what to discard. Whatever values and principles you choose to live by are a good place to start.

Some people like to guide their lives with goals. Whether you do that or not, it is always wise to guide your life by your values and principles. With every decision I make, I can ask myself, "does this decision bring me closer to (love, honor, trust, respect, service, gratitude) or further away?" I strive to make choices that bring me closer to my principles.

What to Empty First From the Cup:

The things to empty first are the things that we're holding onto that we know are not serving us. These are things like guilt, blame, anger, resentment, regret and worry. In order to let them go, we have to be at peace with them, meaning that we experience them, but choose to not give them time to fester in our soul.

Another area where I choose empty the cup are man-made rules and belief systems that do not serve, or don't serve all the time. What things has society or my past experiences told me to believe, and I've just done so blindly? Why do you believe what you believe? Why do you do what you do? Why do you act the way you act? Is it a conscious decision? Is it habit? Is your life based on principles, or rules? What is your motivation for doing what you do?

Much of our lives were imprinted on us by our environment. Our nationalities, family environment, social/income status, political beliefs all came from where we were born, or from heavy influence from family and friends. How strongly do we attach to these things as being the 'best' or 'right' things? I've traveled around the world and met with a diversity of cultures. I've lived in South America, Europe, and Asia. When I was living in Argentina, I came up with the phrase *solamente diferente*, which means only different. My way of viewing things was not better nor worse. It was only different. When I chose to see things in this way, it allowed me to appreciate the other person's point of view in a deeper way.

The more we think we know, the less we are able to learn. This is attachment to knowledge. When we believe that we know something, then we create filters to support what we know. The stronger our belief in something, the stronger the filters are. This prevents us from expanding our knowledge and gaining additional insight. The more that we can unlearn and empty the cup, the more we can grow and learn at a higher vibration.

The Placebo Effect

The placebo effect is well know in the medical arena, but it's used all over the place. A placebo is a story we tell ourselves that changes the way our brain and body works. This is a way that the brain organizes and creates a place of safety. We tend to accept the things that align with our framework and beliefs, and reject those things that don't. In a sense, we create our own perspective of reality.

The placebo effect is a great example of the power of the mind. People can be given sugar pills and feel better, believing that it is a medical treatment. The more that we can intentionally master the power of the mind, the more that we can influence both the mental and physical aspects of our lives.

Seth Godin wrote an eBook called *Stop Stealing Dreams* that includes concepts on the placebo effect and how it affects us in our daily lives, especially as it pertains to marketing. These are some highlights.

One source of the placebo effect is confirmation bias. This is when we expect something to happen, so we filter ourselves to look for that thing to happen. When we expect to have bad things happen to us, it's amazing how much they do happen.

Confirmation bias also occurs each time we make a decision. For example, after we buy a new car, how often do we see that car show up? All of the sudden, we see everywhere. Since we start to see so many of them, we believe that we must have made a great choice. This is confirmation bias. It also happens when we choose to believe something. We create filters that support what we believe and discard what we don't believe. This is the danger in attaching too much to knowledge. We may be discarding new information that will serve us well, just because it doesn't fit with our current set of beliefs.

Another source of the placebo effect is comparison, when we make a judgment for A to be better than B. When this happens, we look for evidence to support our opinion. This is also part of attachment, which will be discussed later in the book.

A third source of the placebo effect is affiliation. This is when we establish our join a group. This group can be anything from a government organization or company, to a motorcycle or athletic club. It may be people that drive Chevy trucks or that wear Nike shoes, or anything else where we see an affiliation.

Another form of the placebo effect is ritual. This is when there is a physical transaction with someone else. If we receive a sugar pill from a doctor (someone in authority), it has a better impact than if we received it from someone not in authority.

Being aware of the placebo effect, and gaining a better understanding of the power of the mind, will allow us to understand what stories we are telling ourselves, and what reality we are creating for ourselves. If they benefit us, then use them. If not, let them go.

PRINCIPLE 2
STANDING IN YOUR POWER

*"We are all like buckets of water with holes in it,
only we don't know we have holes. The water is our power/
potency/authenticity and the holes are where we are giving
away that power unconsciously."*

Time and Energy, The Only True Currency, and Our Power

*H*OW POWERFUL ARE YOU? Do you even know? How are you using your power? What does it mean to stand in your power? Where are you giving away your power?

Time and energy are our only true currency. They are the source of our power. We exchange our time and energy for everything else in life. We invest it in our jobs, our families, and our hobbies. We use it to develop our skills and talents. We spend a lot of time exchanging it for money to buy other things. It is the only currency we have, and once spent, we can't get it back. It can only be spent in the here and now. ***Our past has created residual value based on our experience, but we cannot exchange it for something*** *unless we spend time and energy here and now.* In your work experience, the amount of success that you've had in the past can help dictate the price you will charge for your services, but the only way to make that amount would be to work and provide service in the present. The past is nothing more than present moments where you chose to invest. You can't go back and change it. You can only change the present.

By the same token, you can make plans for the future. You can create goals and dreams, but the only way to make them come true is by spending time and energy towards that goal now.

We can use our power (our time and energy) intentionally and consciously, or we can use it reactively through programming. Sometimes, our programming is a more efficient use of our time and energy. Our brain has figured out how to do some things on autopilot that increases our productivity. For example, when we first learned to drive a car, we had to be very conscious of every aspect of driving. After years of driving, sometimes we will drive from home to work, and wonder how we even got there, because we've trained ourselves to almost automatically drive. At other times, however, our programming depletes our time and energy with no added value at all.

Intentionally making decisions that empower you is one of the most important ways that you can be authentic and show self-love and love for others. To stand in your power means coming from a place of love and making empowering decisions, even if they are difficult. It also means accepting responsibility for your decisions.

We will discuss this in great detail in the next chapter.

We give away our power when we choose to blame others, instead of accepting responsibility. We give away our power when we act or choose not to act based on what we think others will think of us. We also give away our power any time that we act out of fear, where fear really isn't warranted (i.e., possibility of bodily harm, death, etc.).

Another way that we give away our power is by giving our decision-making power to an external organization without thinking through the ramifications of that decision. This is common with religious organizations, government, and corporate jobs.

Examples of giving away our power include:

- Acting or not acting out of fear of what somebody else will think (or more accurately, our perception of what they will think)

- Getting angry, sad, depressed, etc. because "they made me mad" (placing the blame of your emotions on somebody else)

- Tiptoeing around others, and believing that you are responsible for their actions, reactions and emotions

- Blindly doing whatever a government, employer, or any other authority figure tells us to do

- Doing things strictly out of habit, instead of being intentional about it

In order to stand in our power, we must first create an awareness and recognize where we are giving away our power. Reacting instead of responding is one way to recognize this. Another way is to contemplate where we get defensive or where we may act unreasonably emotional. We all have triggers that make us react unreasonably. This points to an area within ourselves that we get to explore and release.

There are various types of energy. For this discussion, we will focus on mental and physical energy. Our mental energy is where we create things. Our physical energy (including our words) is where we bring things to reality, based on our actions. It is important to realize that the more you are able to focus with your mental energy, the more quickly you can materialize in the physical world. If you are trying to focus on dozens of things at a time, then your effectiveness becomes like a shotgun, where little pellets are spread over a wide area. If you discipline yourself to focus on just a few things, then you become more laser-focused and more effective and efficient with your time and energy.

One area where we give away our power is when we choose not to decide. This usually happens when there are two or more good options to choose from. The downside of indecision is that, while you're in a state of indecision, you're not using your time and energy towards any decision. If you just make a decision, and focus your power towards that decision, you will be further ahead, even if the decision wasn't the best one. A good decision that you execute on is better than the best decision that you don't decide on.

Motivation does not create action. Action creates motivation. When we choose decisions of action, it is in the action that creates the motivation. When we act, dopamine is released in the brain, which helps provide motivation. If you ever don't feel 'motivated' to do something, just start, and the motivation will come.

Another interesting aspect of time is that not all time is valued equally, due to the ebbs and flows of our energy. For example, I'm more productive in the morning, so I plan the big tasks to get done in the morning, and the less important things in the afternoon. Also, some people feel less productive with different weather, seasons, etc. As you evaluate your life, you can determine when you are most productive and when you are less productive, and plan accordingly. When you realize that you have highs and lows in energy and productivity, you'll also have less of a tendency to get down on yourself in those moments that are less productive, and just accept them as part of your ebbs and flow. You'll also find that you get just as much done when you allow yourself to flow. You can get a lot further swimming downstream than swimming upstream.

Here are recommendations to maximize your effectiveness and efficiency:

1. **Identify and leverage your high-energy times -** Some people are more effective during the morning. Many people slow down right after lunch. Some people are less effective during winter or rainy seasons. Whatever patterns you may have, identify them and then maximize those times when your energy is highest.

2. **Single-task everything** – Focused multitasking is a myth. Sure, you can take a shower and brush your teeth and think, because tasks like showers have become habits and are on autopilot. When you try to multitask on important things, you really only focus on one thing at a time, and pay a 'switching tax' for every time you switch. For focused tasks, you can only focus on one thing at a time. Use your calendar to block out specific times for specific tasks and focus only on that task during that time period. Eliminate all distractions like email, social media notifications, and anything else that might distract you. You'll be amazed at how much you can get done in a short time.

3. **Create habitual routines** – For years, I have had a morning ritual that consists of exercise, prayer/meditation, reading, journaling, and a few other things. These small things build up over time. I can't tell a big difference in going to the gym between yesterday and today, but I see a huge difference between today and a year or two ago. These fundamental routines not only help us in the long term, but they fuel our energy on a day-to-day basis as well.

4. **Narrow your focus** – In today's world, most of us take on too much. We take on too much responsibility. We buy too many things that require our attention and time. We don't know how to say no. This diffuses our focus and reduces our ability to be successful. Identify one or two key things you can focus on.

For example, at work, what is the single most important thing that you could do to have a dramatic impact? Do that thing. In your personal life, what are the one or two things that are out of balance? Focus on those things so that, over time, something else is your weakest link, and you can move your focus there.

5. **Reclaim any energy/power you are giving away** – Most of us are like water buckets with lots of holes in them. We have holes from worrying too much about the future, thinking too much about the past, worrying about what others think of us, being victims to our thoughts and emotions, and many other things. We spend mental cycles in fear that could be better spent in action. As you evaluate your daily activities, look at areas where you are using your power in ways that do not serve you, and make the decision to focus that energy in more productive areas.

When I first started this journey, I didn't realize all of the places where I was giving away my power, especially to other people. I thought I was just being a nice person. I was a people pleaser. I didn't speak up or share my opinion, even many times when I thought it would add value. I didn't realize how many habits that I inherited growing up that I thought were normal. By creating an awareness of the concept of standing in my power, I was able to evaluate where I get to reclaim that power. I still have a long way to go, but I've come a long way.

Standing in Our Power with Our Words

Words are interesting tools. We give them whatever meaning we were taught. If we were taught that a word has a bad meaning, like a swear word, we give it a label as a bad word, and associate a bad feeling with it. Whenever somebody says a swear word, we may even feel a cringe of resistance, or judge the other person.

Our words are part of our creation process (think, say, do). Anything that is created follows this pattern. We think up an idea. We start to share it, either written or verbally, and through our actions, we bring it to reality. We can choose to use empowering words or disempowering words. We can give away our power in the words we use. Here are some examples of disempowering words that we might have been using out of habit, with their corresponding empowering word:

- *I have to* vs. *I get to*, or *I choose to* (i.e., *I have to* go to the store) – In this example, by saying *I have to*, it sounds like someone is making you do something. In reality, you don't *have to*, you *get to*.

- *I can't* vs. *I choose not to* (i.e., *I can't* play the piano) – If you really wanted to play the piano, you would commit to lessons and practice. If you don't play the piano now, it's because you have chosen not to make it a priority in your life.

- *You made me angry* vs. *I felt anger* (placing blame instead of accepting responsibility) – The only person that has any control of your emotions is you. You can, however, choose to give up your power to your emotions and to the other person, but that is still your responsibility, not the other person.

- *I am angry* vs. *I felt anger* (separating our emotions from who we really are).

- *This is the truth* vs. *this is my point of view* (closing ourselves off from other points of view).

When we fully accept responsibility for our thoughts, feelings and emotions, we should allow our words to reflect that as well. Nobody can make us angry. It is a choice we make. Also, when we can separate who we are from our thoughts and emotions, it allows us to further the distance from them. When we say we feel anger, instead of saying that we are angry, we create a distance between our authentic selves and the emotion. This allows us to better evaluate if it will empower us or not.

Sameness vs. Better or Worse

In her book *Choosing Clarity*, Kimberly Giles illustrates an amazing principle that helps us stand in our power. It is the principle of value and sameness. This principle states that you believe that your intrinsic value never changes. You are whole and complete as you are. You are always amazingly valuable as a being, and nothing can change that. When you believe that, then you also believe it about others. You are no better nor worse than anybody else. This means that in your communication and actions, you are the same as the President of the country, or the person sweeping the streets, and each person should be treated with the same respect that you treat yourself.

Many times, we give away our power to somebody in author-ity because we believe that they are better or more powerful than we are. We are afraid to speak up in meetings if we have a differing opinion. When we realize our sameness, it allows us to stand in our power. It also makes us a more valuable employee because we are not afraid to speak up if we have a differing opinion than someone in authority.

Helping Others Stand in Their Power

If we are parents or in a leadership position, we can help or hinder our people with standing in their power. If we have a tendency to be over-controlling, other people may show up as victims. If we feel threatened when some-body starts to change and stand in their power, it may be challenging for us to support it. On the other hand, if we empower our people with a clear understanding of their responsibilities, and then allow them to perform their duties, even if we believe we can do it better, they will learn to stand in their power and perform at a higher level.

Many people naturally give their power away to authority. It's something we've been taught by our parents, teachers, government and religious organizations. What most of us were not taught is that we can show respect towards these people and groups without giving away our power. We can disagree with others and still be respectful. We do not always have to say yes to somebody in author-ity if it does not feel right for us. Hierarchy within an organization is another area where we may be hesitant to question authority. Just because a manager says something does not mean it should not be questioned. True, they may have ultimate authority within the scope of the job, but questioning something that you have doubts about could be beneficial to the company. There are many examples of people who do things within a company that they would never do in their personal lives. Recent bank scandals come to mind as a great example of this.

There are two pieces of empowering advice that I give my clients who are working in corporate jobs. This advice provided me with a powerful perspective when I was working corporate jobs. The first thing is to always remember that you really work for yourself. There are many people that feel like they are slaves to their jobs. If they take the position that they work for themselves, it is a more powerful way of thinking. The second piece of advice that I give is to create a 'go to hell' fund. This is money that is set aside that can support you for at least six months, so that any time you go to work, and have had enough of the situation, you have the freedom to tell your boss to 'go to hell,' and walk out. Even if you never use the fund (which I haven't), you create a huge amount of freedom and power by having this fund available.

Daily Ritual and Standing in Our Power

One of the key things that this book emphasizes is creating a daily ritual of self-investment. This can include things like exercise, prayer/meditation/mindfulness, reading, journal writing, gratitude, and service. These will all be covered later in the book. It is important to understand that a daily ritual of self-investment is one of the most powerful things we can do to be authentic and stand in our power. I do mine first thing in the morning, and it prepares me to have a powerful day. This showing of self-love and self-respect is the single most important part of my day.

Morning Pages Exercises:

- How effectively are you using your time and energy? What are three simple things you can do to reclaim your time and energy for more productive things? Are you willing to do it?

- When during the day is your energy the highest? Are you planning the most important activities when your energy is highest? What can you change in your schedule to use your energy more productively?

- What daily ritual do you already have in place? What can you add to it to make a change in your life?

PRINCIPLE 3

COMING FROM A PLACE
OF LOVE

THE TWO GREAT GIFTS — LOVE AND CHOICE

THE GREATEST GIFTS we have as humans are the power to love and the power to choose. The greatest combination of these is the decision to choose to always come from a place of love. Love is always the correct response. If all humanity did was live from this principle alone, the entire world would be a better place.

In life, there are two opposing forces, or motivations—love and fear. In the Greek language, there are four types of love: eros, filos, storge, and agape. Eros is a physical, romantic love. Filos is a fraternal (sibling) love. Storge is an empathetic type of love, Agape is a universal love, or a love and caring for all people, including ourselves. For the purpose of this book, and as a guide in your life, I wish to use the definition of agape, unconditional love. More than a feeling, agape is a motivation and understanding.

When we make a choice out of fear, we limit ourselves immensely. We are afraid of making mistakes, so we don't choose anything. Gandhi said that freedom is not worth having if it doesn't include the freedom to make mistakes. My advice is to make lots of mistakes, just don't make the same mistake twice. People choose to act out of fear when they're afraid of what other people think.

Love drives us forward. Fear moves us backward. Love is always the correct choice. This, however, is not as easy as it is stated, as there must be a balance between love for others, and love for ourselves. At times, people sacrifice their love for themselves for the love of others. This tends to place them in a 'victim mode.'

Gaining a True Understanding of Unconditional Love

Love tends to have different meanings to different people, based on their life experiences and influences. We learned about love from the people that surrounded us and taught us. They learned love from their experiences. Somebody who grew up in a warm, loving, nurturing home has a completely different experience of love than somebody that grew up in a home with physical, emotional, and/or sexual abuse. Some parents showed love at all times, where others were more conditional. Movies give us a false meaning of what love is. If we were raised in an abusive family, our perspective of love can be skewed. If we were loved conditionally, we really don't understand the depths of love.

Unconditional love is just that, unconditional. It loves

and accepts all things in all people. It realizes that every person is on their individual paths, learning their lessons. It believes in the best in others, knowing that we all have our foibles and missteps. It does not judge or compare another's path with their own. It realizes that our strengths can be another's weaknesses, and vice versa. It believes that everyone is doing their best at wherever they are along their path.

Thich Nhat Hanh said, *"Understanding someone's suffering is the best gift you can give another person. Understanding is love's other name. If you don't understand, you can't love."* When we gain an understanding that the negative actions of other people are out of programming and fear, we can have compassion and be caring when they need it most. This love is accepting, unconditional, compassionate, and boundaried. With agape, we love because of who we are, not because of who the other person is.

In most cultures, we equate love with a feeling or an emotion. In the Greek language, the word agape is more of a motivation. It's why we do things. The 'feeling' of love may or may not be there, but the motivation of unconditional love is there. It doesn't depend on who the other person is or how they react. If it did, it would be conditional. We love others because of who we are, *not because of who they are*. Our giving of love is our responsibility. How it is received is not our responsibility.

Balancing Love For Yourself With Love For Others

Truly loving ourselves is the biggest task of our existence on earth. When we were born, we came into this world as love. But as we grew and were influenced by family, friends, education, corporations, and the media, we were filled with fear and shame. We were taught that we needed to protect ourselves from pain, and we needed to be safe, so we created a shell and we created our own version of how the world was supposed to be. We put up walls of fear to protect us from this pain and keep us safe. We began to filter everything through a filter of fear. "What if I get hurt?" "What if nobody picks me?" "What if she leaves me?" "What if I get fired?" By looking at life with the filter of fear, everything became scary, and we painted our true selves into a tiny, safe, pain-free corner. But that's not working. We are hurt more by the fear of pain than any actual pain itself.

It's nobody's fault that this happens to us. The people around us are doing their best to help us, but it's our brain that is trying to keep us safe, so it creates these stories of how dangerous it is out there. It wants to keep us safe. Most of this fear-based programming was created before the age of seven, when our judgment and decision-making skills were that of a child.

When we realize that we can shed all of these imaginary walls that we have created, that pain is just energy, and that we are safe, then we can let love shine through. We can be our true selves and experience the whole range of life and emotions. We don't have to go about life protecting ourselves from others. When we release our fear walls, we get a glimpse into our magnificence that has been hiding beneath, just waiting to be seen and expressed.

Loving ourselves unconditionally means that we love

all sides of ourselves as we are, here and now. That doesn't mean that there aren't aspects of ourselves that we wish to improve, it just means that we accept where we are on our path. It's easy to love the things about ourselves that we like. It's more challenging to love our deep, dark secrets that we hide away. They are part of us as well, and they have served a purpose. When we learn to love all that we are, we can love others in the same way. We can only love others as much as we love ourselves.

In the Christian Bible, one of the great commandments is to 'love thy neighbor AS THYSELF.' This means that there should be a balance of love for self and for others. The more we learn to love ourselves, the more we learn to love others.

Coming from a place of love means that when we make a choice, we make it based on a balance of love for ourselves and love for others. When we come from a place of love, we are serving our purpose. Let me repeat that. When we come from a place of love, we are serving our purpose. When you act out of love and compassion, you are serving a higher purpose.

This balance is so important. If you love yourself without being balanced in love for others, you may become selfish and egotistical. If you love others without having a balanced love for yourself, you may fall into the martyr or victim mentality, doing everything for others and sacrificing yourself. This balance should always be evaluated as you come from a place of love.

It's rare that someone is balanced in their love for self and others. Ask yourself if you're leaning too far in the area of self-love or the area of victim/martyr. Based on my experience, most people are lacking self-love. How do you balance the scales? What can you do to love yourself more? What can you do to invest in yourself? Are you comfortable alone in the quiet?

You are the most valuable resource that you have. You cannot buy another you. As you learn to love yourself more, you will grow in love for others. A good barometer for how much you love yourself is how comfortable you are with yourself, by yourself.

Here are some questions you can ask yourself about your self-love:

- How positive and loving is my self-talk?

- How well do I treat my mind, spirit, and body?

- How much do I look to external sources for validation and love?

- How much do I believe I have to defend my beliefs and actions?

- Can I admit when I am wrong or when I don't know something?

- Do I feel safe?

- Do I feel loved?

- Do I blame others or do I accept responsibility?

- How do I invest in myself to show love for myself?

Also, ask yourself these questions regarding balancing love for self and love for others:

- When I have to make a decision between showing love for myself or love for others, what steps do I take to decide which decision to make?

- Do I always give in to the will of other people because I'm afraid of what they will think of me? Do I always have to have my way?

As you spend time answering these questions, you may gain insight into areas for improvement. Don't judge yourself. Just look at the opportunities to love yourself more and be balanced in your love for others.

The more we love ourselves, the more accepting, forgiving, and compassionate we are towards ourselves and towards others. As we learn to love ourselves more deeply, we care less about the opinions of others. We learn to stand in our power and our authenticity. We become ambassadors of love, peace and service. As we become the change we wish to see in the world, the world changes.

Love vs. Fear

There's a lot of talk about authenticity and empowerment and life purpose. Here is a beautiful yet brutal lesson I have been blessed enough to experience. When we are afraid, we do not show up with sustained authenticity and power. If we are terrified of being hurt or abandoned or misunderstood we are not free to be our truest selves. Fear and anxiety keep us small and in survival mode. We will do, say, and even BE something that is a complete betrayal of ourselves in order to feel and stay safe. We are biologically hard-wired for survival at all costs, including the cost of our soul's expansion, delight, and purpose. If we are in

*relationships, jobs, circumstances, and dynamics where we
are afraid, we will not step fully into our power and truth.
We will sacrifice our spirits to stay "safe" in our physical
lives. The first step is to be completely honest with ourselves
about where we are in fear. If it is inside us then we must
commit to heal however we can. If it is outside us we must
shift our actual circumstances. When the fear is healed, the
authenticity will be right there ready to ROAR! May each
one of us have the strength to free ourselves from being held
hostage to fear.* – DAWNI ANGEL

Love unites, fear divides. Love strengthens, fear weakens. Love pushes forward, fear retreats. The more we live in love, the more expansive our reality. The more we live in fear, the more limited our possibilities become. Living in love changes our whole perspective on life.

In our lives, our thoughts and actions come from one of two places; love or fear. One of the most common fears that people have is our fear of what others think of us. We all want to be liked and to belong. We don't want to hurt others. When we worry about what others think of us, for the most part, it isn't really what other people think of us, it's our *perception* of what they will think of us. When we choose to stop caring about what we believe others will think of us, we reclaim power.

This principle really hit home when I was coaching a client. He brought up the issue of his dog pooping on his neighbor's lawn. He was always worried about what his neighbor would think of him if he didn't go over and clean it up, so he did. I explained to him that the actions might be the same, but if he changed his motivation from fear of what his neighbor thinks, to love, it would change everything for him. If he chose to come from love, he would clean up the dog poop anyway, because it is the responsible thing to do, and it's what he would want if he were in the other person's situation. When our motive is love and not fear, we act out of a place of accountability and responsibility, and not out of fear of what others think of us.

We can care about others without caring about what they think of us. What they think of us has to do with their programming, judgments, etc. It has nothing to do with us. We get to choose to stand in our power, come from a place of love, and act authentically, instead of acting out of fear. Walt Whitman said, "Life doesn't give you the people you want, it gives you the people you need: to love you, to hate you, to make you, to break you, and to make you the person you were meant to be." Each interaction with another human being gives us an opportunity to learn to be our authentic self and stand in our power.

Not caring about what others think of us does not mean that we should discard everything that others say about us. There may be hidden gems of truth in what they say about us. They may see something in us that is currently a blind spot to us, something that we do not yet see in ourselves. As we listen to the opinions of others about us, we can listen with an open mind, then ponder on their words to see if we feel there is anything that is worth exploring more deeply in ourselves.

I heard someplace the saying that 'your opinion of me is none of my business.' It's true. What you think of me has nothing to do with me. All of your opinions are based on your experiences, which created filters around all of your interactions with people. For example, if you were abused by three people, and all of these people had tattoos, then you might associate tattoos with abuse, consciously or unconsciously. There is no wide validation of this thought, but for you, it would be your truth. Your opinion of me has nothing to do with me and everything to do with yourself. If we can choose to love ourselves and act out of love for others, it will expand our possibilities, because we will cease to worry about the opinions of others. Eliminating this one limiting belief can change your life forever.

Fear is a lack of understanding. Whenever something shows up as fear, if we examine it closely enough, it is because there is something that we don't understand. Many times, a fear comes up because we don't understand the magnificence of ourselves and our capabilities. The more we learn to love and understand ourselves fully, the less we will fear. It's not that the fear goes away completely, but that we choose to give it less of our power.

Fear keeps us from chasing our dreams. Our brains are trained for survival, protection, comfort, and safety. But that's not where the fun is. I remember the first time I went skydiving. I was not fond of heights, but it was something I always wanted to do. As we climbed to 14,000 feet, my body was filled with excitement and fear. My heart was pounding, and I wondered if I could really make the jump. It all came down to the commitment I had made with myself to skydive. When I jumped, after the first second, my fear was gone, and there was only pure exhilaration. I was living 100% in the present. I was free of the fear that had gripped me so tight. When I opened the parachute and soared high above the ground, there was a sense of peace and satisfaction.

The key that I have learned is that the fear of the thing is greater than the thing itself. The mental anguish that we choose to put ourselves through is a waste of time and energy. It's all made up. If we can choose to make a commitment to something, and keep our energy on the commitment, it helps us alleviate the fear that might show up. If fear is the only reason you can find not to do something, then do that thing. When you come to the realization that the fear is imagined, it is easier to lay aside. In the movie After Earth, the character played by Will Smith said this:

> *"Fear is not real. The only place that fear can exist is in our thoughts of the future. It is a product of our imagination, causing us to fear things that do not, at present, and may not ever exist. That is near insanity. Do not misunderstand me, danger is very real, but fear is a choice."*

One of the most powerful ways to change the way we see fear is through *reframing our reality*. This is true with other emotions as well. Due to our upbringing and programming, we have given negative and positive charges around our emotions. This is true with fear. It has been shown through research that if you can reframe fear as excitement, it takes away much of the charge, which allows you to push through those things that you fear in a much easier fashion.

How Do You Like Your Cage?

Believe it or not, we all live in our own cage. We get to choose how big the cage is by our belief system. The question is, what do we believe our cage is for? Most of us create a cage to provide us safety from the outside world, but it ends up limiting our freedom. We don't see it as limiting us, but as protecting us. Some of us have larger cages than others, but it's still a cage.

We can decorate this cage, make it look pretty, include all the latest fashion and technology, but it is still a cage. It keeps us from living an expansive, free life, greater than we can even imagine.

What is this cage? Some people call it our comfort zone. It's where we feel safe. It's where things are predictable. It's the stories that we create in our head, the model of how life should be for us. It's the rules and programming that we received from our parents and friends growing up, from our education, our country, our government, and the media. It's the things that we were taught were 'normal' and 'acceptable.' Our cage is built from fear.

In order to expand the cage, or even eliminate it, we get to push the boundaries of the cage. We have to become uncomfortable. When we realize that the freedom found outside of our current cage is so much greater than the illusion of safety where we are, we will choose the discomfort of expanding our boundaries for greater freedom.

Is there something you see that is currently outside of your cage? Is the only thing keeping you from it your fear? If your fear were not there, how would you achieve what is currently outside of your cage? That's the thing you should do.

The only limitations we have are the ones we place on ourselves. That is our cage. Choose to get uncomfortable, test your limitations, and overcome them.

Accepting "What Is" as a Part of Unconditional Love

Accepting yourself and others as they are is a huge aspect of unconditional love. Wanting yourself or someone else to be different than what you are right here and now is conditional, and fighting against reality. Improving yourself should always be a quest, but should not cause internal conflict just because it's not occurring exactly when or how you want it.

This is especially true in regards to others. Many times, we believe somebody should be different, or that they're not progressing fast enough, being kind enough, etc. We are measuring their progress with our yardstick. Think about how selfish that is on our part. By imposing our thoughts and expectations on them, we believe our way is better than theirs. We are wanting to take away their freedom to walk their own path in the way that they believe is best.

Accepting what is also reduces a lot of stress and resistance in our lives that doesn't add any value. When we create expectations of how things should be, we tend to punish ourselves for the gap between our expectation and reality. When you think about it, it's kind of silly. We just made up the expectation, and then we get down on ourselves when our made up story doesn't happen. It's like looking at an orange and saying it should be a banana, just because you said so.

It is common human tendency (or programming) to resist. We resist pain, change, when things don't go our way, being uncomfortable, and a host of other things. These things are temporary. Resistance only intensifies the effect of these things. When we accept them, instead of resist them, we get through them faster and easier.

How do we know when we are resisting? When we feel open and relaxed, we are accepting. When we feel closed and tight, we are resisting. When we feel frustration, anger, disappointment, we are resisting.

Believing that everything that happens in your life is for your benefit takes trust. Looking for the good, or for what can be learned in every experience requires trust that the Universe or a Higher Power (whatever your belief system is) has a higher perspective than you do. As I look back on my life, many of the most challenging times I had are also the most endearing, because it was during those times that I learned the most about myself. It's when I grew the most. It's when I learned compassion for others in difficult situations. It was part of my hero's journey.

Accepting "what is" creates one of the most freeing and empowering ways to live. So many times, something happens, and we create resistance to it. We think that something shouldn't have happened, or we wish that things were different. If something has happened, any resistance is futile. It won't change what already happened, so it is a waste of time and energy. When we choose to accept what is, the resistance goes away, and we are free to choose how to proactively respond to it, instead of fighting against it.

Coming From a Place of Love and Courage

The Latin root of courage (old French, *corage*) is *cor*, or heart. True courage means coming from the heart, or from a place of love. Courage allows us to stand in our power, and to come from a place of love instead of fear. Fear is overcome by courage, or the heart.

Most of us spend way too much time in our heads instead of our hearts. The more time we spend in our heads, the more opportunity there is for fear to be fabricated. As we learn to listen to our hearts, and act from there, the better our decisions will be, and the more we will come from a place of love. How do we come more from our heart? One way is to quiet our minds and be present. This can be done through meditation, mindfulness, or just taking a few deep breaths on a regular basis. When we realize that we have thoughts, but we are not our thoughts, it allows us to stand in a place of power. If we just recognize when fear-based thoughts enter our mind, we can quickly dismiss them as not serving.

It takes courage to be open and vulnerable, to show our weaknesses as well as our strengths. It takes courage to give up the need to protect ourselves from pain and the illusion of not being safe. It takes courage to stand for what we believe, regardless of the consequences. It takes courage to give up the illusion of control, to allow the Divine to take a prominent role in our lives.

By coming from a place of love, and creating boundaries, we become extremely courageous. Knowing where we stand gives us confidence. Not being tethered by fear that we have fabricated gives us freedom to explore the boundaries of our soul.

PRINCIPLE 4

THE POWER OF CHOICE AND MEANING

Power of Choice

AGENCY, OR THE POWER TO CHOOSE, is one of the greatest gifts that we have. Even in the most confined circumstances, we still have the power to choose. As Victor Frankl illustrated in his book *Man's Search for Meaning*, "Everything can be taken from a man but one thing: the last of the human freedoms—to choose one's attitude in any given set of circumstances, to choose one's own way." Between stimulus and response is the amazing power to choose. Will we choose to react, based on programming, or will we choose to respond, based on proactive thought?

Everyday, we get to make a myriad of choices. Some are small, some are big, but each choice impacts who we are. The challenge is that sometimes we have given up making choices simply because we do not realize that we can. We have given up our agency to programming, tradition, or authority, and simply act out of the programming we have created, instead of acting out of our own free will and thought.

Some people choose to be victims, and act like they have no choice, yet this, too, is a choice. Some people choose to play the game of life big, whilst others choose small. We choose to join or follow organizations that align with our beliefs, even when some of what they profess isn't in alignment. Many times, we choose to give up our power of choice when we attach to an organization.

Choice is something we DO, not something we HAVE. Until we act on a choice, it is just a thought. Think, then act, then outcome.

Sometimes making a decision can be challenging, especially when we are choosing between two great options, or really have no idea which choice to make. When making difficult choices, I ask myself these three questions to guide my decision-making:

1. **Is this choice coming from a place of love?** Am I making this choice out of fear or love? Does this choice balance love for self and love for others?

2. **Will this decision empower me or disempower me?** If I make this choice, does it allow me to stand in my power, or am I giving away my power?

3. **Does this feel light or heavy?** Do I feel free or burdened with this decision? This question gets me out of my head and into my heart. So many times in making decisions, we only use our head and our emotions. When we can quiet the mind and listen to our heart, we can receive a more expansive answer. For me, this is the tie-breaker. I will always follow my heart over my head.

If a decision is coming from love, is empowering, and feels light and free, I can move forward with a high degree of confidence that it is the correct choice.

One of the most important aspects of choice is choosing what not to choose. When we say yes to many things, it becomes difficult for us to accomplish everything. We will get into more detail about this in the chapter of essentialism.

The Power of Giving Meaning

Another important aspect of choice is the meaning that we give each choice or anything that happens in our lives. The old phrase "making a mountain out of a mole-hill" means that we have chosen to give something with small meaning a greater meaning for us. We do this all of the time. We get greatly offended by something that somebody said, when it was likely said innocently.

We are great storytellers in our mind. We create stories about things that happen. But many times, these stories are negative and false. Additionally, we collapse what happens, and our stories about what happens, and we believe they are all the truth. This is what creates our perception of the truth that can be vastly different from another person experiencing the same things.

Events occur in our lives, and we make up a story for what they mean. We are taught how to behave by a bunch of made up rules so that we fit in. We are brainwashed with what is acceptable and what is not. We make up our own expectations of what we want our lives to look like, and when they don't, we become depressed because we didn't achieve our made up life.

For instance, imagine you call your spouse or a friend and they don't pick up the phone. Your mind starts to create a story on why they didn't pick up the phone. Are they mad at you? Are they out with someone else? Do they not want to talk to you? You look for evidence for your story, to support it. What happened is that they didn't answer the phone. That's all.

When we create stories about what happened, we create a ton of extra stress that doesn't need to exist. The stress and anxiety only becomes real because we choose to create it. If we can learn to drop our stories and just stick with what happened, our lives become infinitely more enjoyable.

Here's the process of our storytelling:

- Something happens

- It means nothing

- We make up a story about what it means

- The story we make up creates our reality and what is and is not possible

When we can learn to separate what happens with our stories about what happens, it provides freedom. It takes the charge out of the experiences we have because we realize that the only meaning any event has is the meaning we choose to put on it.

Since we are the storytellers, why not create stories that empower us?

PRINCIPLE 5

FILTERS AND PROGRAMMING

*A*LENS CAN HELP US see things better. It provides clarity, or allows us to see something up close, in the case of binoculars and telescopes. When I was eleven years old and I went to the eye doctor. My vision prescription was 20/400, which means severe impairment. When doing eye tests, I had to walk forward from the line to see the big E on top. I drove home with my new glasses on and saw that trees actually had leaves on them, instead of being just a big, green blob. I finally had clarity.

A filter removes things. A water filter filters out impurities in the water. Sunglasses filter out undesired rays and light. Our belief systems function in a similar way as we take in new information. We learn something new, compare it to our vast database inside of our mind, and then categorize it based on our data. If it conforms to our current beliefs, then it is easily categorized as 'truth' to us. If it does not, it may simply be disregarded as untruth. The more tightly we hold to a belief, the more stringent the filter becomes. This is known as confirmation bias. Some filters serve us. Some do not.

Filters are a huge part of what create our perception of life. When we are born, we are born into an environment where our race, economic status, education, and many other aspects are already dictated, and not things we have specifically chosen. When we are born, we don't know that we are Asian, Christian, Democrat, middle-class, or any other myriad of labels that we are born into. We accept these things as who we are through our environment. As we grow up, we take these things for granted, and they become automatic filters for us. We establish opinions about these things, believing they are better or worse, by comparing them to others. We create division around these things, believing that our way is better. We either separate ourselves from those that are not like us, or we try to 'convert' them to our way.

Most of us spend a lifetime defending those labels we are born with, without even knowing why. Our parents, with the best of intent, pass down things that they learned as they grew up. We grow up learning to divide, compare, categorize, to make sense of our world. We are surrounded by authority figures in government, school, and the work-place, and many times, blindly accept what they say as truth.

As you read this book, your filters are helping you decide which pieces to accept and which pieces to reject, based on all your past experiences and programming. As we explore these concepts, I ask that you do so with an open mind. If you don't, you may discard something that could serve you well.

Programming

A computer program is a set of instructions that helps automate performing a specific task. For example, this application that I'm using to write this book contains a program so that when I press the letter A on the keyboard, the letter A appears on the screen. When a program produces the desired result, the code (the computing language) is thought to be good. If I pressed A on the keyboard and the letter Z came on the screen, the code would be bad, because the desired result is not what I wanted.

As humans, we have been programmed since we were very young. Our parents may have programmed us on how to treat adults, how to sit at the table and eat, the 'right' way to do dishes, clean our room, and a ton of other things. In school, we were programmed how to combine letters into words and sentences, how to do mathematics, and many other subjects. We were even taught, like Pavlov's dogs when the bell rang, to go to the lunchroom when the lunch bell rang.

Unfortunately, not all of our programming was good. As humans, we all make mistakes. The programming that we received from our parents and others was based on the programming they received. We were handed down limiting beliefs regarding what was possible and what was not possible. We even created our own programs based on the experiences we had. For example, if we were picked first for a game, we could create a program about how good we are. If we were picked last, we might create a program that says we're not good enough.

Some of our programs served us well for a time, but

then stopped working after a while. As a baby, we cried when we were hungry or needed a diaper changed. Those programs don't work for us today. There were other things that we may have been taught when young, like don't talk with strangers, that today in the business world, wouldn't work as we network with others and make new connections.

Intentional Habits and Unconscious Habits

We are creatures of habit. We do things a certain way because we were taught to do them that way, or because we've created a pattern of doing it that way. For example, fold your arms. Then unfold them. Now, fold them the other way. Does it feel weird? Why did you choose to fold your arms the way you normally do? Is there a rule about how you should fold your arms?

For some habits we've created, we've done so because they are more efficient or effective. Some habits, like exercise and diet, we've consciously chosen or chosen not to do. The question to ask yourself is, which habits are unconsciously programmed, and which ones are intentionally chosen? For the ones that are programmed, are they serving you?

As a simple example, I used to wash my hair three or four times a week. It's what I was taught when I was growing up, so it's what I did. When I was 45 years old, a friend of mine was doing an experiment. He was not going to wash his hair for a month. I thought I'd give it a try as well and see what happened. I wet my hair every morning as I showered (I choose to shower every day, just to wake up), but I didn't apply any shampoo. I have relatively long hair, so I thought it would be a telling experiment. After a month of not washing my hair, I couldn't tell the difference. Neither could those around me. So, I decided to extend the experiment three months. After seeing the results, I now only wash my hair with shampoo four or five times a year, much to the chagrin of shampoo companies. It may not work for everybody, but it does work for me.

After going through this experiment, I started looking at all my habits and asking why I do what I do. Is there a better option? Can I eliminate this habit altogether?

Programming and the Brain

Our brains are magnificent tools. They look to protect us from harm and keep us safe. They avoid pain. They automate tasks so they can be done more efficiently. Our brains allow us to plan our lives, set goals, and achieve whatever we choose to accomplish. On the other hand, many times, our brain goes overboard in wanting to keep us safe. It does this by creating fear; fear of change, lack of control, fear of the unknown, fear of what others think of us, fear of being alone, and lots of other unfounded fears. The programming that creates these types of fear do not serve us. Much of this programming occurred as children, when our decision-making capabilities were not fully developed. This is the programming that covers up our authenticity. This is the programming that limits our growth. This is the programming where we give away our power.

How much of what you have learned is still true for you, or still serves or benefits you? In college, did you still use the same books you used in the third grade? Do you still have training wheels on your bicycle? Are there things that you have believed all your life, just because it was always taken as truth, and never questioned?

Life is a continuous evolution of learning, integrating, and letting go. Unfortunately, many times, we forget the letting go aspect. When we do this, it makes it difficult to learn and integrate new things into our lives.

What does it mean to ask yourself if something still serves? It means to ask yourself if this piece of knowledge or habit still provides value in your life. As we evaluate our fears and our programming, we can determine if it serves us or not. If we realize that it doesn't serve, then we can choose to unlearn that program and create a more empowering program that benefits us.

Another thing that we can do is give our brains new instructions. The current instructions it has are to avoid pain, keep us safe, and help us survive. These instructions are what provides so much fear in our lives. What if we came to a realization that we are safe, that nothing can hurt our true selves? What if we realized that we have made it through 100% of the pain and difficult times in our lives, and that none of the fear, worry, or stress that we had contributed to getting through the difficulty? What if we understood that even the pain that we've experienced provided us with valuable lessons and insight into our lives? Would we be willing to give our brains a break and let it know it doesn't have to work so hard to protect us?

You can make a decision to let your brain know that it can take a break, and doesn't have to work so hard to protect you. It takes conscious effort to reprogram the brain. One way to do this is through affirmations. Some people think that affirmations are hokey, and that's okay. Whether we like it or not, we are constantly using affirmations, consciously or unconsciously. Think about your self-talk. You are affirming something all the time. Unconsciously, our fear programming of failure, of being alone, of what other people think of us and other fears, are constantly running in the background. We can choose to combat these fears with empowering affirmations so that we can neutralize and unprogram limiting beliefs. One method that I use I call the flipit technique. I take whatever the negative thought or fear is, and create an affirmation that is just the opposite. I flip it. Here's an example:

- Fear: I'm afraid of what people think of me.

- New affirmation: I love what people think of me!

Then, after I flip it, I look for reasons to support it. In this example, here are some reasons:

- First, it really doesn't matter what they think of me. That's their business, based on their program. It has nothing to do with me.

- I love having the free agency to think whatever I want. Why shouldn't they have that right as well? I love that they are using their freedom to think how they want to.

- They are using their time and energy to even think about me, whether it be good or bad. I'm honored that they would use their most precious resource on me.

- If they say something to me that might feel hurtful or negative, they may see something in me that I'm not seeing because it's a blind spot for me. They could be providing me with a gift for learning and growing.

As we learn to reprogram our conscious and unconscious negative self-talk and thoughts with empowering affirmations and mantras, we can change the way we see things, because we have changed our thoughts about them.

Triggers

A trigger occurs when there is a negative emotional response to something. We can recognize our own triggers when we have an unusually strong reaction or emotion to something, or when we react without even thinking about it. Take the example of road rage. Somebody tries to move into our lane without seeing us. We get angry, flip them off, and say a few choice words out of anger. This is an automated response for some people. If we were to intently think about the situation, we would realize that nobody is perfect. A stranger would never intentionally try to crash into us on a speeding freeway. It was a simple mistake. We all make mistakes. Why get angry with somebody for a simple mistake? It is an example of our 'fight or flight' programming, where we choose to fight with words and hand gestures.

Many of our triggers are programming from a previous

experience or belief system that gets challenged in a current situation. For example, if I was bitten by a dog as a child, and it was a traumatic experience, I may get triggered whenever I see a dog today. It has nothing to do with the current situation, but our program creates a belief system that is still running.

Learning to stay present and create awareness allows us to create a longer pause between stimulus and response, which allows us to change our behavior. Things like road rage rarely happen to me any longer, and if it does trigger me, I catch it immediately and release the trigger. In fact, I can take pleasure in knowing that an accident was avoided. Also, the person in the other car probably already feels bad that they weren't more careful.

When people trigger us, it has nothing to do with them. For me, when I get triggered, I think of it as a gift, because it gives me an opportunity to look inside of myself for the root cause of the trigger, so I can work on releasing it.

Triggers are something that take time to correct. Many times, we recognize them after the fact. This is still a good thing, because an awareness was created. With long-embedded programming like triggers, we need to be patient with ourselves and with letting them go.

The Path from Slavery to Mastery to Release

As we begin this journey into uncovering our authenticity, and shed away those things that no longer serve us, there is a natural progression. At first, we realize that we have become slaves to the things that take our power. Our thoughts, feelings, filters, programming and attachments have all robbed us of some of our power and freedom to act intentionally. As we become present and look at these things, we determine which ones we want to master and reclaim our power. Once we reclaim our power and feel comfortable with living a life of intent, there are many aspects that we can release.

For example, with the principle of forgiveness, we could be holding onto a grudge because somebody offended us or wronged us. By not forgiving, we are a slave to that grudge or resentment that we choose to hold on to. Once we realize that holding onto this grudge no longer serve us, we choose to forgive and let it go. Not for them, but for us, so we become the master of forgiveness. With time, we come to realize that there is nothing to forgive, because the only way somebody can offend us in the first place is if we allow it. It is our responsibility not to be offended. When we come to this realization, we realize that there is nothing to forgive, so we release the concept that forgiveness is needed in this circumstance.

Another example is that of addiction, which is one form of attachment. When we can't control our addiction, we are slaves and give away our power to the addiction every time we feed it. Then, when we recognize the addiction and choose to master it, we can, but there is still time and energy spent being the master. For example, if I'm an alcoholic, but I've mastered the addiction for the past five years by attending AA meetings once or twice a week, there is time and energy spent going to meetings. If we can come to a point to see where the addiction is an effect, and identify and eliminate the root cause, then we can release the effect. When we get to the point of release, or non-attachment, where nothing triggers us to drink, then we gain more of our power back. There is no charge around drinking.

This path takes time, so be patient with yourself. Awareness is the first step. After that, it's the cycle of recognition of where we're giving away our power, then choosing to reclaim it, whether it's before or after the incident. With time, we can let it go.

It's All Made Up

When you grow up you tend to get told that the world is the way it is and your life is just to live your life inside the world. Try not to bash into the walls too much. Try to have a nice family life, have fun, save a little money. That's a very limited life. Life can be much broader once you discover one simple fact: Everything around you that you call life was made up by people that were no smarter than you. And you can change it, you can influence it... Once you learn that, you'll never be the same. – STEVE JOBS

When you think about it, the vast majority of life is all made up. We divide a planet with visible and invisible borders to create countries. We make up a time system of days, hours, minutes, and seconds. We make up ways to measure distance, like miles and meters. We make up a system of money, and act like it really has value. It's all just a game. We make up the idea that land should be owned, so we just take it from others in many instances (like the

Native Americans). We make up ideas, governments, moralities, and other systems, and then often enforce them on others, even through violence or pressure. We as humans like to put things in their little boxes. We create agreement as humans on how things should be, and then we take them as hard truth. We like the illusions of control and safety.

Many of these made up stories, like time, serve us in a "shared reality," so we can meet with others at a certain time, however coming to the realization that so many things in our lives are just made up allows us the freedom to examine other areas of our lives that might be made up and not serving. In the end, there is so much that is just made up, why not make up stories that are empowering?

There are some things that we as humans have made up that have become outdated, but we still use them. Here are examples:

- **We still measure the power of autos in horsepower**. This is an artifact of when we switched from horses to autos years ago.

- **Eggs are sold by the dozen**. This is an artifact when eggs cost one pence each. A shilling was 12 pence, so you could buy 12 eggs for a shilling. People no longer pay with shillings, but we still buy eggs by the dozen

- **The 8-hour workday**. This is an artifact of the industrial revolution where assembly lines were put in place. At that time, you needed to have everybody there at the same time in order to manufacture automobiles or goods. Today, there are many jobs that don't require this, but still adhere to the 8-hour workday.

- **The education system**. The education system that we have today is a result of the industrial revolution, where assembly lines were created, and they needed interchangeable people, like interchangeable parts. It is a system of conformity. Today, we live in an age of ideas, where much of what we learn in school is rarely, if ever, used.

Once you realize that we live in a made-up world, it provides an immense amount of freedom in how you live. When you understand that your reality is not fixed, but very flexible, then you can reframe reality.

Collision of Programming

When two people get together and are programmed differently, different expectations are created. For example, when I got married, my wife believe that she had to make dinner every night with a new meal. I was used to making a big meal once a week so I had leftovers, so I didn't have to spend time making dinner every night. With cleaning the house, she thought the house needed to look a certain way, different than I did. Since she had these expectations she was pressured unnecessarily by what she thought I wanted. Once we talked about what worked for both of us, she was relieved that she didn't have to cook all the time.

We all have our reality of 'how things are,' based on

how we were raised and trained. When we can release the expectation of how things 'should' be, we can open ourselves to infinite possibilities. We can let go of our attachment to our past programming and look to new alternatives. It may be uncomfortable at first, because we are creatures of habit, but when we learn to embrace change, we will find that there are many ways to do things.

As we interact with others, and become aware of programming collisions, we can talk through them, clarify them, and determine what works best for the relationship.

Choose Your Programming

The important thing to understand about filters and programming is that it is happening all the time. Every time you make a decision, you create filters to support that decision (confirmation bias). It is crucial to understand that, if you choose, you can choose your programming, instead of letting external influences or internal reactive programming make that choice. Our thoughts, feelings and emotions are tools. They are not us. When we come to this realization, we can create a separation between who we really are and them. When we make this separation, we can more objectively evaluate each thought, feeling and emotion that arises and choose to entertain it or not. If we choose not to entertain it, we create a void that needs to be filled. It is at that moment that we get to choose what to fill that void with.

Choosing to come from unconditional love instead of fear is a huge anchor point in choosing our own programming.

Non-Attachment, Non-Labeling, Non-Judgment

Another set of powerful principles of Zenpowerment are the concepts of non-attachment, non-labeling, and non-judgment. By applying these principles in our lives, we gain a whole new level of freedom and perspective. Attachment, labeling, and judgment are all filters which can dramatically limit our perspective and possibilities. These filters are all learned behavior, and can be unlearned.

Non-attachment

Attachment is a program that starts early in life. This phenomenon in the western world is called the endowment effect. As little children, we create a sense of ownership of things. When things are ours, we value them more. Since another one of our primary fears is fear of loss, this only increases the level of attachment to something we take ownership of. The good thing is that this is a learned behavior, as there are other cultures that do not exhibit the endowment effect.

Many people think of the principle of non-attachment only as it relates to material things. While this is a portion of the concept, the aspect that has provided me with the greatest amount of freedom is non-attachment to ideas, knowledge, and opinions. When we form an opinion on something, we attach to it, and it becomes a filter for future information coming to us. We also begin to falsely identify with it, like it is a part of us. When our opinion is challenged, we feel that we must defend it.

Attachment is a form of resistance to life.

An opinion is merely an interesting point of view. It is not who we are, it says nothing about us or others. If we choose to look at our opinions in this fashion, and not attach to them, then there is nothing to defend, and much to learn about how other people think, and why they think that way.

Our choices and experiences create filters, which creates a paradigm. A paradigm is a typical pattern or example of something. One objective of non-attachment is not to create a new paradigm, but to move between them, to gain different perspectives.

As an exercise, find somebody with an opinion that is drastically different than your own, and seek to understand the other person's point of view. You will be surprised how much empathy you can gain for another person, and how much you can learn about a different point of view when you're not trying to defend your own.

Expectations

Expectations are a form of attachment and judgment. When you expect a person to behave a certain way, and they don't, then you become disappointed, and tend to judge that person for not being as you expected. Who are you to say how they should behave? What right do you have to take away another person's freedom to act as they wish?

A simple example of this is the stock market. If a company is expected to perform at a certain level, and it performs under that level, most of the time, it gets punished in the stock market, and the price goes down. Two different companies could achieve 20% growth, but if the expectation for one is 15%, the stock goes up. If the expectation for the other is 25%, the stock goes down.

If we create an expectation with a goal to hit on a certain date, and we don't achieve on that date, we tend to be disappointed. Why? Are we perfect in predicting the future? It seems pretty absurd when we think of it in these terms. It's great to have goals, but it's also beneficial to remember the journey and not just the goal.

When we can accept that any expectation is made up, and it is more powerful to accept what is, then we can choose to reclaim more of our power.

Attachment to knowledge

"The truth you believe and cling to makes you unavailable to hear anything new." – Pema Chodron

Attachment to knowledge is another form of programming that limits our growth and development. When we attach to knowledge, we put filters on that supports our knowledge, and filters away learning that doesn't support it. This is called confirmation bias. It filters out anything that doesn't support your initial belief or knowledge. But what if your initial belief was faulty?

In the Christian scriptures it tells us to become as a child. I believe this is especially important when it comes to knowledge. A 5-year-old doesn't act like they know everything. They are curious. They ask 'why' about everything. As adults, we can use knowledge that serves us, but we should be careful not to attach to it. Even the contents of this book. If they serve, use them. If not, discard them. Each person's interpretation of 'truth' is subjective. There are principles and laws that we currently cannot argue with, like gravity, but the majority of things are our interpretation of them. The less we attach to knowledge, the more we are able to learn.

Addiction is a form of attachment

Addiction is an obvious form of attachment. We all suffer from some type of addiction. Some are sometimes viewed as more severe, like drugs, alcohol, gambling, sex, or smoking. Others may include addiction to things like gaming, TV, mobile phones, social media, approval from our spouses or children, or addiction to food. Some people are even addicted to noise, so they don't have to deal with the quiet in their mind. For some of these items, like smoking, there is an addictive chemical hook aspect, like nicotine, but the mental and psychological aspects are far greater than the chemical hooks. What these things have in common is that they are things outside of ourselves that we use to avoid pain, search for pleasure, create a feeling of safety, or just to escape.

But escape from what? Avoid what pain? One recent theory is that addiction is created due to a sense of lack of connection (for more information, see this article in the Huffington Post www.huffingtonpost.com/johann-hari/the-real-cause-of-addicti_b_6506936.html?). This is a lack of connection to ourselves and to others. Our society is programming us to focus more on things than people.

This, in turn, requires us to work longer hours, many times in isolated cubicles.

Creating loving connections with ourselves and others will allow us to reduce addictive behavior to things outside of ourselves. When we realize that we are enough, and that we have everything we need inside of us, we will stop looking outside of ourselves. When we choose to love and serve others, we will make meaningful connections with those that matter to us.

Non-labeling and Non-judgment

"There is nothing either good or bad but thinking makes it so." – Shakespeare's Hamlet

Labeling and judgment are things that help our rational mind categorize things. Unfortunately, many labels and judgments contain an energetic charge with them that can create emotions which may lead us to act irrationally. Labels such as good/bad and right/wrong also may be circumstantial, which means they cannot always be counted on. The power that comes from not labeling is that it brings a power of acceptance. Additionally, labeling and judgments, specifically as it pertains to people and groups of people, are too general, and do not take into account each individual. Labels and judgments only create division, which comes from fear.

When we label something, then we tend to judge it and create an energetic charge around it. For example, if we label something as bad, then we create a judgment that creates resistance around it.

What if we dropped all labels and judgments and just accepted things as they are? What if we came from a place of love at all times, and then determined if something empowered us or not? If it empowered us, we could consider it or integrate it. If not, we could simply discard it.

Labels divide

Labels create racism, sexism, wars, and creates an 'us versus them' mentality in the world. We label and judge people all the time by the clothes they wear, the way they look, the car they drive, and a myriad of other things. We categorize and put them in boxes because it makes us comfortable.

There is a story I will paraphrase here, called "Is that so?" There was an old man in a small farming village in China in the 1930s. One day, he was given a horse as a gift. The whole village came by to look at the horse, and said, "isn't this a wonderful thing?" The man simply replied, "Is that so?"

A couple weeks later, the man's 16-year-old son was riding on the horse and it bucked him off and broke his leg. The people in the village remarked, "Isn't that a terrible thing?" The man replied, "Is that so?"

A week later, the military came through all of the small villages to draft all of the able-bodied men to go to war. Since they boy's leg was broken, he couldn't go. Shortly thereafter, all of the men in the village that had gone to war were killed. Since the boy hadn't gone to war, he survived. The people in the village proclaimed, "Isn't that wonderful that his leg was broken?" The old man simply replied, "Is that so?"

The story goes on, but the moral of the story is that labels create filters that serve no purpose. Something that may be perceived as bad at one instance in time can be perceived as good in another. If we choose to be grateful for all experiences, and not label them, our lives become much richer.

I had a similar experience a few years ago. Within an eight-day period, I was involved in two separate accidents, in two separate cars, caused by deer. In one of the accidents, I hit a deer on the freeway and it caused about $3,000 worth of damage to my car. When I took the car in to be restored, I had noticed that it was leaking fluid that looked like a mix between oil and antifreeze, so I let the mechanic know of my observation.

When I went to pick up the car after it was restored, I talked with the mechanic about it. He asked me if I had recently changed the oil in the car. I let him know that I did so about two weeks before. He let me know that the oil plug in the engine was loose and was about to fall out. If I had not hit the deer, and my oil plug came out, it could have drained the oil and frozen up my engine, which would not have been covered by insurance, and would have cost about $5,000, instead of the $500 premium I had to pay with my insurance. In this case, it was good (label) that I hit the deer, to avoid a more costly experience.

Comparison and Competition as a Form of Judgment or Labeling

Comparison and competition put us in a mindset of labeling or judging one person superior or inferior to another, in one specific area of life, like a sport. While they can be tools to make us improve ourselves, the comparison against others could be damaging as well. There can only be one first place. Does that mean that everybody else is not good enough? What if we place too much emphasis on winning? When we don't win, are we a failure?

As we look at competition, as in all other aspects of life, there should be a balance. A powerful objective within the realm of competition is to improve the self, not necessarily be better than others.

Working together for a goal, however, instead of competing, comes from a mindset of abundance. It comes from knowing that as we contribute and collaborate, even with our competition, we make deposits into the karmic bank account that is abundantly overflowing with whatever we choose to put into it. There is power in working together.

Observation vs. Judgment

Observation is the ability to notice things. It is the way we perceive things. Judgment occurs when we attach previous knowledge and emotions to what we observe.

Non-Attachment, Non-Labeling, Non-Judgment Are Not Absolutes

While understanding the principles of non-attachment, non-labeling, and non-judgment are extremely valuable tools, they are not absolutes. We will still attach, label and judge, but in a very different manner. Being aware of these principles will also help us realize how many of them are learned behavior, or programming, that we learned as we grew up. If we were raised in a homophobic family, our perception on homosexuality is very different than if we were raised in a gay family. If we were raised in a vegetarian family, our experience around food would be different than a family that had BBQs every weekend. If we were surrounded by a religious or political environment at home, we would see things differently.

Being aware of these principles will allow us to choose, and not be chosen upon. The biggest questions I ask myself when looking at something I've judged, labeled, or attached to is, "Does this serve (or does this work)? Does this position empower me? Does this unite or separate? Does this feel light or heavy?"

Take the example of a dimmer switch on a light. With a dimmer switch, you can set the light to all levels of brightness. Are any of them right or wrong, good or bad? No. There may be a time when a different level of light serves better than another. For example, if I lose a contact lense on the carpet and need to look for it, having the light at its brightest would serve best. If I wanted to have a romantic evening at home with my spouse, a dimmer setting would serve best.

Looking Outside of Yourself

Are you looking outside of yourself for stability, safety, or love? Do you say to yourself, *"I'll be happy when...?"* If so, please stop. It's not out there. It's inside each one of us.

Almost everybody I know has the program "I'm not good enough" running to one degree or another. For this reason, we begin to look outside of ourselves for something to make us 'good enough.' We look for a job, house, spouse, or car that makes us believe that we are better in the sight of others. We go to schools for prestige, join influential organizations, or associate with brands (think Harley or BMW) to raise our perception of our self-worth. The truth is, we are all good enough, right here, right now. We don't look at a little baby and think that they are not good enough because they haven't learned to read or drive a car. They are perfect, whole and complete, just as they are. So are we. When we choose to reprogram ourselves by eliminating expectation, comparison, and whatever other filters may be limiting our belief about ourselves, we will see that we have everything we need here and now. When we are able to do that, we realize that we are good enough, and that the concepts of stability, safety, and love are inside of us, and can only be found inside of us. When we realize that we don't have to look outside of ourselves for these things, we find peace. A flower doesn't look at the flower next to it to compete with, it just blooms.

Our task is to rewrite the story that we have in our head, so that we know that we are good enough. Nobody has gone through the exact same life experience as us. We are the #1 expert in our experience. That means that we are uniquely qualified to make a difference in the world by using our experience and being our authentic selves.

Who We Really Aren't—Emotions, Feelings, Ego, and the Body

Do you know who YOU really are? Are you your body? Are you your thoughts? Are you your work or your family? When you get down to the essence of who you really are, what is it? Is there a separation between your ego and yourself?

I went through an experiment years ago and realized I wasn't my body or my emotions. That was groundbreaking. When I realized that I'm driving around a 1966 Randy Scott as a body, I gained a new level of freedom. When I think of who I really am, I am not my body or my emotions or even my thoughts. I am not the car I drive or the house I live in. I'm not my job. I'm really not anything on this physical plane of existence. When we can let go of these things as attachments, we become free and empowered.

Spend some time meditating on who you really are. What is it that makes you you? What makes you unique? If you were to lose your job, your home, your arm, would you still be you? Are you your thoughts? How much could you get rid of in your life and still be you? If you died, would you still exist?

As you ponder on these things, you begin to get an idea of who you are. There is magnificence in understanding this, and realizing that no external force can touch you, unless you choose to give up your power to that force.

There are several aspects of who we think we are that really aren't even us. These aspects of 'us' need to be observed, evaluated, and separated, so that we may get to the essence of who we are. These things can be valuable tools for us, like clothes and a car, but they are not who we are. As we look at some of these things, you may feel some resistance and hesitation, because we have so closely identified ourselves as being these things. We see no separation. At some points in time, we allow these things to drive our behavior more than we allow who we really are to be in charge. This is not an easy journey as we strip away those aspects of 'us' that we identify ourselves with so closely.

Developing Emotional Intelligence with Zenpowerment

Emotional intelligence (EQ) is our ability to identify and manage our emotions, and interact with the emotions of others in a productive manner. It's how we get along with others, while being empowered and using our voice. It's really hearing somebody, not only what they say, but how they say it.

In this world of email and texting, face-to-face interaction is decreasing. When we're talking face-to-face with somebody, we don't get an emoji if someone is feeling defensive, anxious, angry, or any other emotion. We get to use our perception and intuition to know best how to navigate our own emotions and the emotions of others.

Zenpowerment principles teach how to empower ourselves while being authentic. Understanding our emotions, programming, and filters is key to developing our emotional intelligence.

We Are Not Our Emotions

Emotions and feelings are powerful forces. They bring us joy, sadness, pleasure, pain, excitement, and a myriad of other experiences. The key is this; we **HAVE** emotions and feelings, but we are **NOT** them. Just like we have clothes or a car, but are not those items.

The dictionary defines emotions as a natural instinctive state of mind deriving from one's circumstances, mood, or relationships with others. I would like to take this definition a bit further. Emotions are tools, just like a mobile phone or a shovel. When we can separate our true selves from our emotions, we can learn to observe them and determine how to best use these tools. When we identify our true selves as the observer of emotions, we have a better chance of not giving away our power to our emotions, and becoming their slaves by acting out on them.

Emotions should be experienced and not suppressed. This does not mean that you have to act on the emotion, but merely experience it. There are no wrong emotions. Some people will feel guilty about having a 'negative' emotion, so they feel guilty about it or suppress it. There is no benefit to this, and it is actually damaging, as it can build up over time and cause us to explode. If we take time to experience an emotion as it comes up, we can evaluate it and determine how it might serve us (as a tool), or if we should let it go.

Another important thing to remember about emotions is that they are a form of communication. Each emotion vibrates at a different frequency. If we are tuned in, we can feel it, just like a dog can sense fear. When we get angry, the people around us can sense that we are angry. There are also collective emotions. If a group gets angry, it's a riot.

We should acknowledge and experience all of our emotions, and not hide or compartmentalize them. We can experience emotions without acting on them. We can choose how much time and energy to focus on the emotion. It is in our best interest to experience emotions as our servants, and not our masters. This means that we should rule ourselves, and not allow our emotions to rule us. Being able to experience emotions without having them rule us is a key principle.

Using Emotional Triggers as Teachers

We all have emotional triggers. Triggers such as fear of failure, guilt, abandonment, lack of safety and fear of not belonging are common to all of us. Many times, especially in communication with others, emotional triggers make us become unreasonably defensive or emotional. When we recognize these triggers, we can be assured that it is not the current situation that is causing the trigger, but a deeper set of programming that is not even related to the current incident. We can learn to minimize or eliminate these triggers by doing the following:

- **Recognize the trigger**. By staying present, you can create an awareness so that when you are triggered, you recognize it. Immediately, once recognized, you can minimize the impact of the trigger by realizing that it is a trigger, and not acting on it in an unreasonable fashion.

- **Identify the source of the trigger**. Once you are alone in a quiet place, grab something to write with and ask yourself where was the first instance in your life where you felt like you did when you were triggered.

- **Identify the belief about the trigger**. When you've identified the source of the trigger, ask yourself what you believed about yourself at that time. Many times, this belief is something like, I'm not good enough, I don't belong, I'm not loved, etc.

- **Ask yourself if your current belief serves you, and is really true**. If the behavior from the trigger doesn't serve you, then it doesn't make sense to keep it. Most times, this initial belief is not true, and was established as a child, where our decision-making skills weren't the best.

- **Create a new belief**. If the current belief that creates the trigger doesn't serve you, create a new belief that does serve you. Make it an empowering statement that you can believe.

By going through this process again and again, we can eliminate triggers and programming that don't serve us. This will allow us to better understand and manage our own emotions. Once we understand our own emotions, we can better interact with the emotions of others.

Developing Emotional Intelligence with Others

Yogi Bhajan said, "If you are willing to look at another person's behavior toward you as a reflection of the state of their relationship with themselves, rather than a statement about your value as a person, then you will, over a period of time, cease to react at all."

When you realize that your emotions and triggers are your responsibility, then you can also realize that the emotions and triggers of others are their responsibility. There is no need for you to react to their emotions. What you can do is help them through their emotions by using these tools:

- **Get their communication and be present.** When you are in a conversation or a meeting, and someone is acting defensive or unusually emotional, true two-way communication stops. The other person simply wants to be heard and validated. They want to be talked off the ledge. When this happens, just acknowledge how they are feeling. You do not have to agree. You do not have to defend your own opinion. Just listen and acknowledge what they are saying. Many times, this will allow them to calm down and realize that they might be acting unreasonably.

- **Come from a place of love and empathy.** Since you've realized that you have your own bag of emotional triggers, it allows you to be more compassionate and empathetic when someone shows up with their own bag. One way to look at it is when the other person is triggered, they are afraid. Fear is one of the root causes of our programming that causes triggers. If you realize that they are afraid in that moment, take extra care to show them love and empathy.

- **Postpone a conversation, if necessary.** At times, if a person is really triggered, it makes sense to just postpone a conversation. Communication is two-way; a giving and a receiving. When a person is triggered, they are not in a place to receive communication, so the conversation becomes futile. Wait until there are calmer heads, so you can really address an issue.

How Emotional Intelligence Gives us the Edge

By understanding our own emotions and the emotions of others, we can better understand the importance and impact of communications. It allows us to become more empowered and not be a victim to our emotions or the emotions of others. People around you will notice how you handle heated conversations, and they will respect you for your integrity in difficult times.

Emotional Bank Accounts: The Concept of the Nickel and the Dollar

As we serve others on a daily basis, there is an essence of a virtual currency, and there is a feeling of reciprocity associated with this virtual currency. Everything we do has an energy around it. Likewise, each person has developed, or was blessed with, certain gifts and traits. Because the things that we have been blessed with are so easy in our lives, we take them for granted. By the same token, things that are easy for others may seem difficult for us. This is where the concept of the nickel and dollar came from.

This concept mainly applies in the area of service, where no actual currency is exchanged.

As an example, my skills are in marketing, business management, training, and communications. They come easy to me. I provide lots of value in these areas. On the other hand, I am terrible at typical handyman stuff, like working on cars, fixing up houses, etc. For me to provide someone with business consulting is an easy thing. It's a nickel. For others without that skillset, it may be perceived as a dollar. Here is where the incongruence lies. When we think of reciprocity—if I feel like I'm giving you a nickel, and you feel like I'm giving you a dollar—there is an imbalance in the scales. You feel like you own me a dollar, when I feel like you would only owe me a nickel, if anything at all.

By the same token, if I give you something that I feel is valuable, like a dollar, and you receive it like a nickel, I'm going to feel unappreciated, like you didn't see the real value in what I was giving. In the Bible, this is the analogy of casting your pearls before swine.

This principle can be used in various ways. Here are a few examples:

- In a spousal relationship, a spouse may value something as a dollar when for you, it is easy for you, or less valuable. If you are able to make dollar deposits into their emotional bank account, and it only costs you a nickel, then you both reap a benefit.

- At times, you may be providing service to others that they believe is super-valuable (a dollar), and you do not (a nickel). If it is not communicated to this person that something is easy for you, they may feel indebted to you for a dollar when the contribution on your side was a nickel. This is valuable to understand when providing charitable service where nothing is desired in return.

As we evaluate our interactions with others, it is valuable to consider not only our point of view, but the other person's point of view as well, so we can balance out the scales. That is not to say that if we are giving something that we value as a nickel and they value as a dollar that we should take a dollar's value from them. Instead, we should help them understand what is equitable for both sides in this barter of karma. Also, when somebody offers something to us, we should be empathetic to their point of view and do our best to understand the value with which it was given.

Regulate the Cause, Regulate the Effect

Emotions are an effect. We feel our emotions because something caused them. Additionally, we get to choose the amount of meaning, and thus, the amount of impact these emotions get to have on us. What happens to us is not as important as how we respond to what happens to us, and how we react to what happens to us is in proportion to the amount of meaning we give it. Byron Katie said "The meaning you put on someone's action is what hurts you." It's not the action itself, but the meaning you give it.

For example, if we choose to get offended by the actions of somebody else, that is our choice. We also get to choose how much offense to take, how much time to spend focusing on that, and thus, the amount of anger or resentment we feel. If we get to the very root of it, we chose to be offended. If you make another choice, not to get offended, you also choose to remove any anger about the issue, as well as save all of the precious time wasted on being offended and getting angry.

Programming of Safety

Many people take the conservative path in life, believing it is safer. The concept of safety is a grand illusion. We don't know how or when we are going to die. We don't know when the next accident will happen to us. Sure, there are steps you can take to be more or less safe, but real safety lies in knowing who you really are. There is an immeasurable peace and solace that occurs when you know that nobody can really do anything to you.

It's the brain's job to protect us, to keep us safe. Unfortunately, it's gone overboard. It's like a parent that won't let a child do anything out of fear it might get hurt. The good news is that we can tell our brains to take a break because we really are as safe as we can be.

When you look outside yourself for safety, you are giving up your power. If you fail to take action because it is the safe thing to do, you are giving up your power. Living a 'safe' life is living a small life. Where there is much risk, there is also the potential for much reward. Living a life of risk is living a large life.

When I was 33 years old, I totaled a motorcycle coming down a canyon. I spent months recovering from broken bones. After I was fully recovered, there came a key moment in my life. I could either stop riding motorcycles, out of fear of what happened to me, or I could buy another motorcycle and do the thing I loved. I chose to ride again. When we make our choices out of love, they are more powerful choices, even when they appear more risky.

Knowing That You Know

There are three aspects of knowing; knowing what you know, knowing what you don't know, and not knowing what you don't know. For example, if you are a chef, you know that you know how to cook. You also know that you don't know how to perform brain surgery, as you have not gone to school for that. The biggest mysteries are the things that we don't know that we don't know. We are simply oblivious to them. These are items in our subconscious. There are others in our lives that might see these things clearly in us, and yet we're not aware of them. From time to time, knowledge in this area comes into our awareness. This is when big shifts can occur in our perspectives and lives.

Even when we know something that we know, we should not attach to it too strongly. When we attach to our knowledge, the opportunity to grow that knowledge gets diminished, because we filter out anything that doesn't align with our current knowledge or belief system.

Authority as a Filter

Authority is an area in which we can give away our power. It is also a filter for how we see ourselves and others. Authority can be in the forms of government, our jobs, family, or a group with which we associate. When we attach to authority, we tend to believe all that they say, and lean on their understanding above our own. Also, when we give our power away to authority, many times, we give away our responsibility as well. Atrocities are done by individuals in the name of governments or corporations, that an individual would never do on their own. History is replete with leaders like Hitler and Jim Jones, who persuaded people to give up their power and blindly follow their leadership, ultimately to the death of others, and some even themselves.

Part of the challenge with authority is that it is made up of people who are fallible. Another aspect is that there are people who choose to abuse power. Finally, just because an authority has a number of things that resonate with us, they may not all resonate, yet we tend to accept their position, based on authority.

Expectations as a Filter

Creating expectations almost always causes misery. Expectations are a form of comparison. "This is how it should be." When things don't end up as they *should*, it causes misery. It also causes resistance to what is, because it *shouldn't* have turned out like that.

The problem with expectation is that they are made up. We are predicting the future on how things should turn out. This is dangerous, especially in relationships, where there may be two different sets of expectations. Rarely are they the same. We use our expectations as filters on how people should behave and how things should turn out, instead of accepting them as they are.

When we choose to let go of expectation and accept things as they are, we reduce any resistance of how things should be.

Creating Agreement Instead of Expectations

In the business world and in relationships, creating agreement instead of expectation results in understanding and accountability. Creating agreement requires good communication between parties. If expectations are not clearly communicated and agreed upon, then it only causes misery and frustration.

Creating agreement is straightforward. Here is a suggestion:

1. Agree on specific outcomes

2. Agree on how these are to be achieved

3. Agree on how the outcomes will be measured

If these agreements are written down, then you can refer back to them at a future date, so there is less opportunity for misinterpretation. If you don't write them down, then you're just going by memory, which is fallible. There may be a need for negotiation between parties, but when you can clearly define outcomes and how they'll be measured, there is less room for misunderstanding.

Principles vs. Rules

I have found that guiding my life with principles instead of rules has served me best. These are lenses that provide clarity for me. A principle is something that is enduring, and that applies at all times. The principles that I choose to guide my life are:

- **Love** – For me, love is always the correct response. This is unconditional love. It has always served me. I don't have to love the actions of myself and others, but I can show them kindness and love as a fellow human being.

- **Respect** – This is having a sense of deep admiration for self and others. One of the things that helps me have respect is making the assumption that everybody is doing their best, based on their life experience.

- **Honor** – To me, honor is adhering to a code of conduct. My code of conduct may be different than yours, but it is living with integrity to the code of conduct one chooses. Also, I believe it is in recognizing the divine in myself and others.

- **Trust** – Trust is having faith or a firm belief. Trust is the most fallible of these principles, because trust can be broken by self and others. Once trust is broken, it may be regained through our actions.

- **Service** – Providing service allows us to get outside of ourselves and our selfishness.

- **Gratitude** – Gratitude is the all-natural antidepressant. When you focus on what you do have and what you're grateful for, you realize how blessed you really are.

All of these principles need to be balanced between self and others. For example, if I show love towards others at the cost of my self-love, then it doesn't work. If I show love for myself without the regard of others, it doesn't work. When I use these principles as anchors in my life, I have an immense amount of freedom and direction in how I treat myself and others.

Rules apply in certain circumstances, but not in all. There are times when rules do not serve. In American society, there is an abundance of rules and laws that enslave us instead of provide freedom. People blindly follow these laws and rules, just because society or the government chose to create them.

An example of this hit me early one morning as I was heading to the gym at 5 a.m. On the way to the gym, there are about six stop lights. In general, stop lights are great to regulate traffic, especially when there is a lot of traffic. At 5 a.m., however, there is no traffic, so I have gotten into the habit of stopping at the light, and then proceeding through the red light when there is no traffic. There have been occasions when I would encounter a car at this time of the morning, and I would watch them wait until the light turned green. While waiting for a green light at 5 a.m. is not a big deal, it exemplifies the concept of when a rule serves and when it doesn't.

All principles have natural consequences. Most rules have consequences, but they are man-made. As you evaluate which rules serve you and which don't, you should also weigh the cost of the consequence. A simple example is speeding. If you speed, and get caught, you will get a ticket. If you get too many tickets, your insurance will increase. You don't get a ticket every time you speed. If you speed within a safe rate, there is minimal increase in danger. The benefit of speeding is that you get to your destination faster. With this information, you can determine if the benefit of speeding is worth the cost of getting caught.

You can take this example even further. How could you reduce your chance of getting a ticket? Say the average ticket costs $100. You could purchase a radar detector for $140. If the radar detector saves you from two tickets, then it will pay for itself.

PRINCIPLE 6
ESSENTIALISM

*"Perfection is achieved, not when there is nothing more to add,
but when there is nothing left to take away."*
—ANTOINE DE SAINT-EXUPÉRY

*"The richest man is not he who has the most,
but he who needs the least."*
—UNKNOWN AUTHOR

"If you have more than three priorities, then you don't have any."
—JIM COLLINS

IN GREG MCKEOWN'S BOOK on essentialism, he says that the basic value proposition of essentialism is this, "Only once you give yourself permission to stop trying to do it all, to stop saying yes to everyone, can you make your highest contribution towards the things that really matter."

What really matters to you in your life? Family? Money? Status? God? How others perceive you? Your job? Contributing to a cause? Your body? Your friends? Your intellect? Your hobbies? Social media? Your own personal growth? There is an unlimited list of things we can focus on, but we have two limited resources; our time and energy. Are we investing our time and energy in the things that WE choose matter most, or are we giving away our power to let others use our time as they wish? Are we so diffused with our time and energy that we become a jack-of-all-trades, and master of none? Do we even know how we're spending our time?

Why do we value the things that we do? Is it because it truly matters to us, or is it programming that was instilled in us when we were young?

As someone who has spent his career in marketing, I have been able to see both the light and dark side of marketing. To me, the light side of marketing has to do with understanding customers and their needs and aligning your company's unique value proposition with the customer's needs, and clearly communicating to them.

The dark side of marketing has to deal with pandering to people's insecurities, their longing to belong, to fit in, and to be loved. It uses the customer's feelings of 'not being enough' to get them to buy a product, so they feel good enough, loved, etc. This is an area of my profession of which I am ashamed. Knowing this, however, has given me great power in making decisions. We are bombarded with tons of advertising and news (programming) each day, that tells us we have 'arrived' if we are driving this car or wearing these clothes.

When we are aware of this, we are then able to look at our decisions more objectively, to decide our value and meaning on something, instead of what somebody else tells us. We do not need anything or anybody in our lives to be 'good enough.' We don't need to amass tons of material things around us to 'find ourselves.' In fact, the opposite is true. The more that we strip away the things that don't matter, the more freedom we will find.

The same is true of our time. The busier we get, the more opportunity there is to sacrifice the great for the good. Whenever we say yes to one thing, we are saying no to something else.

When we choose intentional love instead of fear, it becomes a life of essentialism, a life of simplicity. When coming from love, we just need to make sure we have a balance of love for self and for others, and create the appropriate boundaries in our lives. When we come from a place of fear, then we choose to battle the imaginary dragon, with all of its programming, attachment, judgment, labeling and division.

A life based on principles such as love, honor, trust, respect, service, and gratitude is an essentialistic life because you don't have to worry so much about rules. You don't worry about what other people think of you (which comes from a place of fear). You spend your time and energy focusing on those few things that really matter on your life path. With your focus on love for yourself and others, you forge a path that not only lifts you as an individual, but the entire human race.

Minimalism is Just One Aspect of Essentialism

The concept of minimalism has started to gain substantial traction. With things like tiny houses and a more eco-conscious mindset, more people are getting tired of all of the materialism in the world, especially in first-world countries. Contrary to what the media, movies, and marketing are telling us, having more things does not create more happiness. When we search outside ourselves for happiness, we will always be disappointed. There may be moments of joy when buying the new car or next new gadget, but they are fleeting moments.

When we choose to have less material items to clutter our lives, we have less to worry about. We also need less income to support our lifestyle, which means we can do more of the things we really are passionate about. Money is a great tool. It makes a powerful servant, but a terrible master. Most of us can live on much less than we currently do.

The good thing is that there are no rules to minimalism. It is an individual choice. Even in a family, there will be differences in defining personal minimalism. When I got married, I was living a very minimalistic life on my own. I had no kitchen table, no couch, and slept on a futon on the floor. My soon-to-be wife had gotten out of a divorce a year earlier, and was struggling as a single mom of two boys. She was somewhat minimalistic, some by choice, some by circumstance, but she did bring some furniture into the relationship that I chose not to have when I was single. I now have much more in my house than I did previously, but there is no attachment to it, nor upkeep on my part.

The same thing can be done with the clothes you wear and the food you eat. People like Mark Zuckerberg and Steve Jobs were known for wearing the same type of clothes all the time because it gave them less decisions to make. Food choices can also be simplified. This is also an individual choice. While I can eat the same things over and over, my wife likes more variety than I do.

Another benefit of minimalism is the reduction of waste. Every week, I see my neighbors take out their trash, brimming to the top of the can with waste. We take our trash can out once every four to five weeks.

When we declutter our lives on the outside, we also are able to do so on the inside.

My luxuries are my motorcycle and my electronic piano keyboard. They are my hobbies. I get very nice ones, and only pay cash. Same with my work needs of a good laptop and phone. In my home office, I don't have a big desk and chair. I choose to sit on the floor on a meditation mat. The great thing about minimalism is that you get to choose how it looks for you, and what will serve you best.

Whatever type of minimalism you choose, it is also important to keep in mind non-attachment to any material items you have. Be grateful for them, use them well, but always remember that they are replaceable.

Being "Too Busy"

In American culture, being excessively busy is almost looked at like an aspiration. We equate being busy with being important. This is a trap in which many executives find themselves. The unfortunate thing is that being busy usually involves tactical items, instead of the important, strategic items.

The thing about being too busy is that you spread yourself too thin. When you say yes to one thing, you are saying no to something else, and many times, that something else is more important. You cannot effectively prioritize your time if all your time is allocated.

Creating buffer time for yourself is crucial. Creating time where you can be alone to think and meditate will pay dividends greater than you can imagine. Allocating and prioritizing time for the things we deem important will allow us greater control of our lives. Time is a resource that, once spent, we can never get back.

Question how you use your time. Who said that we have to work eight or ten hours a day? This is an artifact of the industrial revolution, where you had to have people on an assembly line. Can you get just as much done in five or six hours, if you remain focused? Are there things that you're doing at work that really are not adding value, and you could eliminate? Being busy is not the same thing as being productive. Being a prisoner in a cubicle at work for eight to ten hours a day may not be the best use of your time. What are you trading for your valuable time?

Smoking on It Before Buying Something

In the movie *Dances With Wolves*, Kicking Bird, a young brave comes into the main teepee to talk with the elders, angry that the white man was coming into their country. He wanted to go kill the white man. The elders of the tribe listened to his complaint, and then replied with, "Let's smoke a while." The elders were wise and not rash to make a decision. They chose to give it time to make a decision, and smoke the ceremonial pipe.

I have adopted the same thing in my life when it comes to buying things or making big decisions. In my family, we have the phrase, "let's smoke on it," which means let's give it some time, and if we still want something in a few days, then maybe we'll get it. This reduces any temptation for impulse items. It has become a good practice.

The 80% / 20% Rule and Essentialism

In Kevin Kruse's book *15 Secrets Successful People Know About Time Management*, he states that successful people follow the 80/20 rule, which is that 80% of the outcomes come from 20% of the activities. He says that successful people focus on the 20% and ignore the rest.

What activities in your life are providing the results you want? How different would your life be if you chose to eliminate 80% of the activities that weren't providing the results you want?

Think of how much time, energy, and freedom we would have if we determined what activities are providing the majority of the outcomes, and simply ignored the rest. Think of how much more successful we would be in those things that we chose to focus on.

The Power of Deciding

To decide something means to come to a resolution in the mind. The root of the word decide means to cut off (de= off, caedere= to cut). This means that once you really decide on something, you cut off all other options.

In 1519, Captain Hernán Cortéz landed in Veracruz. He then commanded his troops to burn the ships. This gave them no other option than to move forward.

How many times in our lives do we make a decision and cut off all other options? How many times do we create a 'back door' or a 'plan B,' just in case? How much more powerful would our decisions be if we cut off all other options? How different would our relationships be if we knew we had to work through all things, instead of opting for a divorce? How much energy would we save if we weren't second-guessing our decisions and thinking of other options?

Another interesting aspect of deciding is that it overcomes fear. If we are afraid of something, and we make a choice, most times, the fear goes away. We're not afraid of the thing as much as we are the deciding.

Indecision is a waste of time and energy because you are not moving any decision forward. You are stalled, and nothing gets accomplished. The faster we can learn to make good decisions, the faster we can move forward with that decision.

As we create a life of essentialism, we should be careful to determine where we want to spend our time and energy. Once we do so, however, we should do it with all of our heart, mind and strength, and cut off all other options. This increase in power and focus will drastically change the results that we get.

Think about your life. What is it that you really want to accomplish? If you have no idea, how many different things can you experience so you can find that thing? Once you find it, what are the activities that will drive success towards your purpose? Are you willing to burn your ships to move forward?

The power in truly deciding will make a huge impact in your life and in the decisions you make from moment to moment.

PRINCIPLE 7

ENERGY AND ONENESS

"Energy flows where the attention goes."
- HAWAIIAN PROVERB

Understanding Energy

Vibrations and waves are not new to us. We take advantage of light waves and sound waves on a daily basis. Think about our senses of sight and sound. We take light and sound waves at various frequencies into our eyes and ears, then turn them into electrical impulses for our brain.

We also use energy waves for a number of things, including mobile phones, microwaves, radio, satellite TV and many other conveniences. These waves are all around us all the time, and we really don't notice them unless we are using the receiving devices (like the mobile phone).

Some animals have a heightened sense of awareness of these waves that is beyond our ability. For example, a dog can hear sound at a frequency too high for the human ear. Bats and dolphins use echolocation to navigate. Interestingly enough, some blind people have adopted a rudimentary version of echolocation, which compensates for their lack of vision.

Physicists have created the superstring theory and M-theory in which they hypothesize that everything is made up of vibrations of tiny supersymmetric strings. That is to say, everything is made up of energy vibrating at different frequencies.

In his book *Power versus Force*, David Hawkins goes as far as measuring the frequencies of different emotions, based on kinesiology. He measures love, peace, gratitude, and courage at a high level of energy, while anger, fear, shame, and guilt measure very low.

Additionally, the Heartmath Institute has shown that the heart has the largest electromagnetic field in our body, about 60 times greater than that of the brain. If we are able to emit frequencies based on our thoughts and emotions, are we also able to receive them? Are we receiving them without even knowing? If a dog is able to sense fear in humans, could we?

The intent of this chapter is not to go deep into the mechanics of energy, nor to tell you how to use all of this energy, because frankly, I don't know. What I do know is that by creating an awareness that everything is made up of energy allows us to explore the possibilities. I do know that I am what some people call empathic. I can sense other people's emotions, to a degree. If you think about it, so can you. Have you ever been in a room or conversation with somebody and their energy lifted you up or brought you down?

Since our time and our energy are our only true resources, are we able to harness energy, or act in harmony with external energy, to gain greater results? Nikola Tesla hypothesized that we could harness the electromagnetic force of the earth and create free power for all. We have already shown that you can harness the waves of the sun to create electricity through solar power. What other waves of energy can we learn to harness? Is it as simple as tuning into the frequency that is being transmitted, in the same way we do a radio or satellite TV? Can we choose to be the receivers?

We are all energy. Our natural state is a state of high vibration, or love, but we lower our vibration through fear, guilt, shame and anger. As we learn to deprogram and reprogram our subconscious, and live intentionally, we can raise our vibration to our natural, authentic state again. As we associate with people of high energy, expose ourselves to books and movies of high energy, we can continually raise our vibration. When we invest in ourselves with habits that improve our lives and increase our understanding of our true selves, we become more enlightened. Napoleon Hill said, "Increase the vibrations of thought to the point where one can freely communicate with sources of knowledge not available through the ordinary rate of vibration of thought." The higher we raise our vibration, the higher levels of knowledge we can access.

Energy of Resistance, Acceptance and Embracing

There is a subtleness of energy that we use that we may not even be aware of. It is called resistance. Resistance shows up every time we have an expectation and things don't work out as we expected. It shows up when we judge something. It appears when we don't want something. It's all over the place, and little by little, it drains our energy. It has become such a part of our everyday life that we hardly notice it. Fear is a form of resistance.

We can learn to notice resistance and let it go. We do this by first creating awareness. Once we notice the resistance, we can either accept or embrace what we are resisting. One common area of resistance is resistance to reality. You might think, *I don't resist reality*, but think about it. Has something ever happened to you and you thought, *That shouldn't have happened*? That's resistance to reality.

As we learn to let go of resistance and become more accepting of reality, we can reclaim our power used in resisting.

Maximizing our Energy

All things are made up of energy, including our thoughts and emotions. When we choose to let go of thoughts and emotions that don't serve, and embrace the ones that do, we become more powerful. When we choose to eliminate limiting beliefs and replace them with empowering ones, we focus our energy in more powerful ways.

In the section on essentialism, we talked about the fact that when we say yes to something, we say no to something else. This is a principle of focus. When we choose to get distracted, our energy moves from one task to another, and our energy is not used efficiently. When we take on too many tasks, our energy gets diffused and we become mediocre at all of them, instead of expert at few things.

When we choose to focus our energy on fewer things, we can devote more energy to them. In the same way that a magnifying glass can focus the rays of the sun into a single point hot enough to burn a piece of wood, when we can focus our energy on fewer things, we can create a focus that provides amazing results.

Our personal energy is not a constant during the day, week, year or lifetime. We have highs and lows, ebbs and flows. We all flow like a river. Some areas are rapids, some areas are slow. If we're rafting down a river, we don't judge the river for how it is. We just go with it. I've realized that I have more energy in the mornings, and so I'm more productive. I plan accordingly. I do my daily ritual in the morning. I plan the big, difficult tasks for the morning when I am at my peak. Then, during the afternoon, I can do the things that require less energy and focus.

Some people find that in some areas of the country and world where winters are harder and days are shorter, they tend to have less energy, and some even get depressed. Some people are less productive during a rainy season. All of these are okay. Being aware of them is helpful in managing your time and energy. Perhaps, where possible, taking on huge tasks is better left when energy is higher.

In the corporate world, we can take advantage of this to make our employees more productive. If there are regular meetings that occur, where people are updated or don't need to be at their peak, plan them for the afternoon. Make it a policy to leave productive time alone so that individuals may focus their efforts when they're most productive.

Understanding that there are highs and lows in our

own personal energy and the energy of others will help us leverage the times when we're most productive, and cut ourselves and others slack in less productive times. As we learn to do this, we'll be surprised in the overall productivity of ourselves and the people we work with.

Oneness

For the purpose of this conversation, I'd like to define oneness as unity and balance. I'd also like to explore it from a few different viewpoints. First, as an individual. Second, in your relationships, and third, from a planetary perspective.

Brain

Let's start talking about oneness from an individual perspective, starting with the brain. There are two hemispheres in the brain. Each of us may have dominant aspects of our left or right hemispheres, but the unity of both sides of the brain is what makes us powerful. We need to have an integration of both sides to function more fully.

The brain is a huge repository of data and stories that we have created. The oldest part of the brain is the amygdala. Its primary mode is our survival and safety. The prefrontal cortex is our rational brain. It allows us to plan, to make decisions, and to manage and filter information coming into it. It connects the dots between our experiences to create patterns. It is also interested in preserving energy, so it changes as many of these patterns into habits to conserve energy. This is also where much of our programming and filters come from.

Body

In the same way that we have separation in our brains, we have separation in our bodies. The three separations that I would like to discuss are brain, heart, and gut. For the most part, especially in the western world, we are primarily driven by our brain, and give little attention to our heart and gut. We basically take information that we have already received to make decisions with our brain. This leaves us with a huge disadvantage. Interestingly enough, our heart and gut also have neurons in the same way the brain does. The stomach is sometimes referred to as the 'second brain' because of the amount of neurons it has. The heart and the gut both send information back to the brain through the vagus nerve. The gut and the mind help the brain in the thinking process. We underestimate how much we can use our heart and gut in making decisions. From time to time, you will hear somebody say 'it just didn't feel right' or 'I followed my gut.' This is an indication that somebody chose to listen to their heart or gut, instead of their brain. Many times, we will get an initial feeling to do something, but then we allow our brains to talk us out of it, normally out of fear.

Our hearts and gut are great guides into the unknown. They do not rely on past data to make decisions, like the brain does. They somehow tap into energy that can provide a higher knowledge for us. I don't know how this works, I just know that it works. As we choose to be led more by our heart and gut, and less by our brain, the world opens up for us in unexpected ways. Making this change from being brain-driven takes practice. It's like tuning into a new channel that has a faint signal. Over time, however, this signal becomes clearer and clearer until it's unmistakable. As we learn to quiet the brain, we can feel the signal grow stronger. That's why meditation and mindfulness are such powerful habits. When we learn to recognize these signals, and not let our brains talk us out of it, we become unerring in our ability to follow our heart and gut.

The Native Americans have a word called *shante ishta* (or *chante ishta* in Cherokee), which means 'the eye of the heart.' They believe that they are to be led by this eye. Their prayers come from this place, and do not need to be spoken. In the Christian scriptures, it says 'The light of the body is the eye: if therefore thine eye be single, thy whole body shall be full of light' (Matt 6:22). I always wondered why it said eye instead of eyes. To me, it makes more sense if it is talking about *shante ishta*. What if we made a conscious effort to be led by our hearts instead of our heads? How would that affect our lives? I've made an effort over the past several years and it has made all the difference.

At times, we have gut feelings that something feels right or wrong. Why do we explain it like that, unless it really is from the gut? Also, there's a phrase 'fire in the belly,' which means we have a powerful sense of ambition or determination.

As we learn to find balance and unity between our head, heart and gut, we become more powerful. Many of the fear-based decisions that we make, solely based on our brain, cease to happen. Opportunities open up for us that we never could have imagined.

Being

In addition to separation of our bodies, we have separation of our beings. This is our body, our mind and our soul. We also need to find balance among these three parts of us. We need to feed and nourish each of these so they may support each other. We can nourish our body through exercise and healthy eating. We can nourish our mind through continuously learning and developing our minds. We can feed our souls through prayer, meditation, and spiritual practices.

We are holistic systems. We like to think we can separate work life from home life, but what we do in one affects the other. It's the same thing with our habits and rituals. If we neglect our bodies and health for too long, it will affect our mental and spiritual capabilities as well.

Planet

I used to prize myself on being an independent, self-sustaining individual. Silly me. I thought I could do everything on my own and didn't need anybody's help. I paid for my own way through college. I got my own jobs. I lived on my own. I felt like I could do anything by myself. Then I realized how absurd this is. As an example, I imagined a little cell in my body thinking like I am, thinking it is all independent, living life on its own, not realizing that it is part of my arm, which is part of my body. For as much as it wanted to think it was all on its own, it was just an illusion.

I realized that I am an interdependent soul connected

to everyone else. I don't grow my own food. I don't build my own house (including the wood needed that is supplied by nature), I don't make my own gas for my car. I didn't create this computer or the internet to communicate with the world. Hell, I hardly contribute anything compared to what I enjoy on a daily basis. Even without anybody else, I am dependent on God or the Universe for the sun, the water I drink and the air I breathe. Take one of those away and I'm dead. I am completely dependent on others to live the way I'm living, and that's okay.

When I got rid of the story and illusion of my separateness from everyone and everything, it made it easier for me to ask others for help and insight. It made serving others easier, because I realized that when I'm helping others, I'm helping the whole.

When we begin to remove the illusion of separateness and realize that we are all interconnected, we get to choose how far down the rabbit hole to travel. There is a physical phenomenon known as quantum entanglement (see en.wikipedia.org/wiki/Quantum_entanglement for an overview from wikipedia), where two subatomic particles (like a photon) were separated by great distance, and then when one particle was spun, the other particle instantly spun in a complementary speed and fashion. Scientists are still trying to figure out how this works, but the implications are astounding. If items are connected, and space doesn't affect the connection, what are the possibilities of connection, and the collapsing of space? How do you detect when two items are entangled?

I remember hearing a story about the various parts of

the body complaining about the stomach. The eyes said, "we have to look all day for food, and the stomach doesn't do anything." The arms and legs said, "we have to walk around and get the food." The mouth said, "I have to eat all of the food." One day, they all decided to go on strike against the stomach. After a few days, they started getting weaker from lack of food. It was then that they realized that the stomach had its contribution as well.

We are not only interconnected to those who are alive today, we are benefitting from the legacy of those who lived before, those who discovered electricity, created the automobile, the many thought leaders that help us to think differently. While they are no longer on this physical plane, we are still reaping the rewards of their pursuits.

Love creates unity. Fear creates division. Oneness is our natural state.

Our ego is not our true self. It is an image that we have made up of ourselves. It's the thing that makes us feel like we're separate, individual. It's the identity that the brain tries to protect, and yet, it's not even real. As we learn to recognize our true selves, and not our ego selves, we begin to also become more aware of our unity with everything else.

Our lives are like an orchestra. Sometimes, we play in harmony with our tribe, our section of the orchestra. Sometimes, we play our own unique melody, standing apart from the rest. Yet, while we play our own unique melody, we are still an intricate part of the orchestra; separate, but not. There is value knowing when to do both. Do you know your melody? Do you know your unique contribution that nobody else can play?

How Things Look for You vs. How They Look for Others

As you raise your energy level, and as you let go of attachment, judgment and labeling, you may begin to look more boring to others. As you delve deeper into a spiritual realm, the things of this realm become less important. You're not worried about the things of the senses as much. The nutritional value of your food is more important than the taste. You realize that that things that you see, hear and feel are, in a large part, an illusion. You would rather spend time delving into the internal journey than to be stimulating the external senses. When you no longer attach to opinions, then the things that others find important, like politics, favorite sports teams, etc., no longer have the same meaning. You may not have anything in common with those people who you affiliated with in the past. Your tribe shifts to those who are also on an individual path of enlightenment and improving the planet. Be prepared for this shift. It is normal for people to fall out of your life, and for new people to come into your life. Your valuable social circles may become smaller, but your circle of influence may become much, much larger.

As you no longer care about the opinions of others, and learn to stand in your own authentic power, you become a lighthouse for others. Some people will admire you. Some people will think you crazy. Just know this, things will change, and will change in astonishing ways.

ZENPOWERMENT
TOOLS AND HABITS

Investing In You

*H*OW MUCH DO YOU INVEST in your job? For most people, it's eight to ten hours a day. How about with our families? How about with our hobbies? Our other relationships?

This body and mind is the only one we get during our ride on this planet. How are we investing in ourselves? I was talking with a friend of mine, and he says he pays a tithing of 10% of his earnings to his church without even thinking about it. He just does it. That got me thinking. How many of us invest at least 10% of our time and energy in ourselves with daily habits that make us better? We have 24 hours in a day. Take out 8 for sleeping, and that leaves us with 16 hours of productive time. Do we spend at least 1.6 hours a day in personal investment? Do we make it non-negotiable? Are we worth it?

If you choose to take on these tools and habits, I can assure you that your life will get better in all aspects. While each of them focus on a different aspect of who we are, using them together will make you more powerful than you can imagine.

Tools

Tools are things we have and can use for good or bad. We get to choose. A hammer can be used to build a house, or to take a life. One of the problems is that, many times, we mistake these tools for who we are. Some of the tools that we confuse with ourselves include our thoughts, feelings, emotions, and bodies. When we can learn to separate our true selves from these tools, we can begin to use these tools, instead of giving our power away to them.

As humans, we are creatures of habit. Some of the habits we've picked up along our journey are great and some are not so great. A habit is an automatic reaction to a specific situation. It's a program. Habits can be created intentionally or unconsciously. The habits that are usually most beneficial are the ones that we implement into our lives intentionally. These habits are valuable tools that help us move towards a particular direction, and assist in changing our perspective.

The habits or tools that we will discuss in this section are:

- Meditation / prayer / mindfulness
- Morning pages
- Gratitude journal
- Affirmations / visualizations
- Service
- Exercise

- Reading 10 pages/day
- Take time to do nothing but think (essentialism)
- Connect to someone important to you
- Plan the important things in your day
- Plenty of sleep, making a request of your subconscious

Each of these habits has power on their own, but together, their power is synergistic, and the sum is greater than the individual parts. Additionally, over time, these habits build residual benefits.

Gratitude Journal

Gratitude provides perspective on what you have. It allows you look at your life and realize the many blessings that have come your way. Being grateful doesn't mean that you are only grateful for the 'good' (label) stuff either. It also allows you an opportunity to reflect on the positive things that come from the trials in life. **Some of our greatest gifts are found on the other side of some of our greatest challenges.** Think of a challenge you are currently facing, or a person you are having a conflict with. Determine why you are grateful for that situation. What can you learn? How can you help the other person?

Gratitude turns what we have into enough. By simply writing down five things you are grateful for every morning, you will change your perspective. They can be as simple or as detailed as you wish. I like to mix it up as much as possible, especially focusing on the most tiny of things, like the intricate design of a butterfly I saw on a hike, or the smell of the bread store as I walked by. Things like sunrises, sunsets, a stranger's smile, and an opportunity to serve all, make it into my gratitude journal at one time or another.

There are so many things that we take for granted as we let our day-to-day programming take over, and we become drones in our routine. When we choose to look at life freshly, like a young child, every day, knowing that we get to write down things that we are grateful for, we begin looking for those things.

As an added bonus, pass on your gratitude list, when appropriate. For the past six years, I have shared my gratitude list on Facebook when I felt it could help another. Many times, I received feedback saying that my gratitude post was just what they needed.

Also, show more gratitude to others in your life. Be grateful for all of the connections you have in your life. A friend of mine who is a gratitude guru even shows gratitude in advance. Whenever she goes out to eat, she gives a pre-tip before the meal order is taken, and expresses gratitude for the service she is going to receive. Then, after the meal, she provides another tip. Needless to say, the service she receives is always superb, and the waiters and waitresses she connects with are positively affected as well.

Meditation / Prayer / Mindfulness

Meditation is the practice of focusing and being present. Meditation takes many forms. It can be sitting quietly in the lotus position, or it can be mindful of the food you are eating. In whatever form of meditation you choose to engage, the important thing is to remember the power of silence and the power of being present. Focusing on your breath is a great way to stay present.

One objective of meditation in Zenpowerment is to create an awareness of who you are and who you are not. If we think in terms of subject and object, we (our true selves) are the subject and everything else is object. Our thoughts, feelings, emotions and experiences are all objects that we get to observe. When we center ourselves through meditation, we are able to separate our true selves from our thoughts and emotions. We are able to objectively look at them to determine if they will serve or not.

Some people prefer guided meditations, some prefer to be alone. The important thing is to make time for yourself. There are also a number of applications that you can put on your phone to do your meditations, as well as record your progress.

Something that I enjoy doing in meditation is picture myself sitting in some thick grass on the side of a clear, slow-moving stream. From time to time, I see a small branch or leaf float by. I picture these branches as my thoughts and emotions. If I choose, I can pick one up and look at it, or I can just let it go by. If I pick it up, I'll evaluate it, and determine if it serves or not. If it serves, I'll set it by my side. If it doesn't serve, I'll gently set it back in the stream to float away.

One of the benefits of meditation is that it helps reduce stress. More than 75% of doctor visits are stress-related, and, according to WebMD, Americans spend more than

$300 billion annually on stress. Other benefits of meditation include increasing emotional well-being and boosting the immune system.

Prayer also takes many forms, depending on your beliefs, but in most cases, it is an act of connecting with the Divine (God, Allah, Great Spirit, Nature, etc.). Many Native Americans would pitch their teepees with the opening towards the east, so that when the sun came up, they could give thanks to the Great Spirit for another day. When we take time to be quiet and make connection with Higher Source, it helps us align with our principles and beliefs.

Prayer is also a great time for reflection and to give thanks.

We discussed mindfulness in the chapter on being present. Mindfulness is gathering more momentum as they are using it to manage chronic pain, PTSD, stress, and anxiety disorders. Learning to stay present without judgment, and just be an observer creates enormous power. Practicing mindfulness on a daily basis increases our peace and allows us to live a life of intention instead of reaction.

Morning pages

We reviewed in detail the practice of morning pages when we laid out the groundwork for this book. For me, morning pages and meditation/mindfulness are the top two keystone habits that makes everything else work. Morning pages is where I do most of my inner work. In order to assist you in your journey, I've included a few ideas of things to write about:

- **Free-flow thought.** This is just letting out whatever is on your mind. Don't edit, don't spell-check, don't stop. Just write.

- **Current frustrations about things that are going on.** Are they real? What's the worst case scenario if they came true?

- **Write down 10 ideas every day for a month or longer.** This could be 10 ideas to help other people, 10 ideas to grow your business, etc. By doing this for an extended period of time, you will create hundreds or thousands of ideas. At least of few of them will be amazing.

- **Breaking through limiting beliefs.** What is the limiting belief? When do I first remember having it? Is it serving me today? What is the cost of this belief? What is a new belief that is more empowering? What can you do to act on that belief?

- Focus on a specific topic that you're interested in, like a blog post or a chapter in a book.

- **What does your ideal life look like?** How does it feel? Get into the details. All things are created mentally and emotionally before they are manifested physically.

- **What are the dark/shadow areas of yourself that you still get to learn to love?**

- **What parts of your ego are not serving you?** What can you release?

- **Review the worst experiences of your past.** Search for the gifts in them, so you can rewrite your story.

- **If you are having huge emotions that you're struggling with, write about them.** What do they really mean? Why are you feeling them? Are they pointing you towards something you get to work on in yourself?

Morning pages are not only a great way to increase your writing skills and creativity, they are a great therapist, and much less expensive than a human therapist.

Service

Service allows us to get outside of ourselves. It allows us opportunity to overcome the ego. When I focus on you, I can't focus on me. In other words, if I'm wallowing in self-pity because I feel like my life is so hard or unfair, the simple act of helping others provides us a different area of focus, and most of the time, makes our challenges feel lighter.

Service also gives us an opportunity to contribute to the greater whole. What I mean by this is that when you are helping someone else, since we are all interconnected, you are essentially helping yourself as well.

Another benefit of service is that it may allow you a chance to gain a different perspective on life. I've had the opportunity to serve the homeless. When you hand someone a blanket on a cold night and they comment, "wow, this is a lot nicer than newspapers," it has an impact on your own life and perspective. When you help someone who is dying of cancer, knowing they only have days left, it makes you appreciate the gift and brevity of life.

As we look for opportunities for service, it allows us to open ourselves to the Divine/Universe and be used as a vessel. When we ask ourselves who we can serve today, opportunities will abound. There are always ways to provide service.

I challenge you to look for at least one opportunity for service every day.

Exercise & Nutrition

When we buy a car, we take care of it by filling it with gas, changing the oil, washing it, and doing periodic maintenance. As our car ages, it may start to break down. Then, we get to decide if we want to pay to have it fixed, or if we want to buy another vehicle. With our body and mind, this is the only one we get. There are no trade-ins. This one vehicle has to last our entire life. How are we treating it? How are we fueling it? How are we keeping it in optimal condition to carry us around for our entire lifetime? We can either choose to invest in our body along the journey, or pay for the medical bills when it breaks down.

We are the experts of our body. We can choose to listen to it. What do I mean by listening to your body? It is using your intuition to know what works for you. It is experimenting on yourself to see what provides the results you want. Sure, there are guidelines you can use, but use them as that, guidelines. For a period of time, my wife chose to be vegan. She was strict with it, and she was miserable. She felt like a slave to the vegan lifestyle.

After a while, she rebelled (against herself) and stopped going vegan. When she started listening to her body, she leaned towards mostly vegan again, but didn't punish herself when she didn't eat vegan.

What we are taught about nutrition may be right, but it may be wrong for us. In western culture, we normally eat three meals a day. For a number of years, I only ate one meal a day and drank mate (a South American tea) for breakfast and dinner. For years, I stayed the same weight. Then, when one of my daughters was born, my wife wanted to lose some post-baby weight, so we both went on a diet. I ended up eating five smaller meals a day, more food than I was eating previously, and lost 26 pounds in a few months.

Another thing to consider is that not all physical issues are created by physical causes. Many physical ailments can be caused by emotional issues. For example, we can hear some tragic news and we get sick to our stomach. Some people hold on to weight as a defense mechanism to feel safe. Once the emotional issue is resolved, then weight falls away. This is another reason to make sure you are creating a balance between body, mind and soul.

Affirmations / Visualizations:

You are already using affirmations, whether you realize it or not. Unconscious affirmations are found in our self-talk. Are they positive or negative? How many times do you tell yourself them, over and over? Some negative affirmations in our self-talk include:

- I'm not good enough

- They won't value my opinion
- He/she won't love me if I say/do that
- I'm too (young/old, smart/dumb, fat/thin, etc.) to do that
- I can't do that because I've never done it before

If you're already using affirmations, why not choose affirmations that are intentional and empowering? If you want to be a new age hippie, just call them mantras instead of affirmations. In the times where negative self-talk comes up, why not replace it with a new belief or affirmation, such as:

- I am of infinite worth
- My opinion is valuable whether others see it or not
- I was made to do this

Affirmations are great for getting us out of a rut and refocusing our thoughts on something that serves us instead of disempowers us. At times when I have a hard time quieting my mind, especially before meditation or going to bed, I'll use affirmations to redirect my thoughts. Some of my favorites are:

- I am love
- I am safe
- I am powerful
- I forgive
- I trust
- I deserve
- I am abundant

When I say these things, I also couple emotions with them. What does it feel like to be powerful? How does it feel to be forgiving? Coupling emotions with affirmations helps anchor them into our belief system.

Some people don't believe in affirmations, and that's okay, but here's a challenge for you. When you're having negative self-talk, create an affirmation that is the opposite, and is empowering. Couple emotion with it and say it 20–30 times and then see how you feel. If it empowers you, create a habit out of it.

Visualizations are similar to affirmations, but they use more of the brain. Visualizing something that we wish to manifest in reality is a type of 'spiritual creation.' We create it in our minds before we create it in reality. For visualization, get in a quiet place where you can be alone and close your eyes. Then, visualize in vivid detail what is is you wish to manifest. Visualize it in the here and now, like you were already living it, or already had it in your possession. How does it make you feel? What does it look like? What are the sounds and smells associated with this visualization?

The more vivid you can get with visualization, the more you can attract that energy into your life.

Reading 10 Pages/Day

Expanding our knowledge is one way to exercise the mind. Just like we exercise and eat healthy to take care of our bodies, our minds need to be exercised as well. Reading at least 10 pages every day gives your mind something to do to improve. Even if you choose to read some trashy novel, it gives your imagination some exercise.

Read things that you are interested in. Read things that fuel your passion. Read things that help you become a better businessperson, spouse, parent, or friend. Read things that stretch your imagination and help you to create new connections between knowledge.

One of my passions is the convergence between science and spirituality. I love learning things about quantum physics and seeing how they might apply in a spiritual realm. When you are able to learn about two things that your are passionate about, and then combine the knowledge, you gain insights that aren't readily apparent to others.

If you read 10 pages a day, you can get through 12–15 average sized books in a year. As a point of reference, the top CEOs read 4–5 books a month, according to Pew Research Center. It's interesting to think that the people that we believe have the least amount of time are those who choose to use significant time investing in their mind by reading.

Take Time to Do Nothing but Think

Many of the greatest ideas in the world have come through contemplation. When the mind is given the opportunity to 'play,' miracles occur. Some forms of contemplation include meditation, prayer, visualization, journaling, and even more active things like walking and yoga. Contrary to popular belief, there is value in daydreaming.

When we step back from focused tasks, we allow and opportunity for our heart, gut and mind to play together, to contemplate the possibilities of the Universe. It is an opportunity to open ourselves to intuition and inspiration and capture those sparks of genius that can be turned into flames to engulf our lives with greatness.

One of these places for me is the shower. Our shower routines are programming that serves us, where we can put it on autopilot and be completely somewhere else in our minds. I get many great ideas in the shower. It's early in the morning when I am more open to inspiration. It's a relaxing environment, except for the last couple of minutes, where I turn the water to freezing and shock myself into a whole new reality. If you've not tried cold showers, I highly recommend it. There are physical benefits that have been documented, but it does something great to you, if you create it as a habit.

Take time out of your busy day to step back and look at the big picture.

Connect to Someone Important to You

We all know that family and friends are important. Most of us know we could do a much better job at staying in touch with people. Whether it is professional or personal, we can all improve our connections.

With social media, it has become much easier to know what other people are up to. On Facebook, we see posts about friends having babies, moving, and even what they had for dinner. Even though we are informed about what's going on in other people's lives, this is not connection. Connection is two-way communication. Connection is showing that you really care about the other person.

Creating a habit of connecting with somebody every day allows you to deepen relationships. It may also provide an opportunity for service, which is another great daily habit. When you make a daily habit out of connecting with someone, it becomes intentional, and not just opportunistic.

Plan the Important Things in Your Day

The more you can focus your attention each day, the more successful you will be. Prioritizing the things that are important to you is one way to focus yourself. It also allows you to be more intentional with your time, instead of reacting to the things that come up in your day.

Choose the three most important tasks that you want to get done during the day. Then, consider when you are most effective with your energy, so that you can plan the important things during your most effective time. I am most effective in the morning, so I make sure that I have no meetings or menial activities planned in the morning, so I can complete my most important tasks during that time.

Your most important tasks should be ones that support your longer term goals, so that you are doing something every day to reach those goals.

Plenty of sleep

How much sleep do you need? Do you know? How well do you know your body? How well do you sleep? General guidelines suggest that 6–8 hours of sleep a night is optimal, but is that optimal for you? Can you hack your sleep?

When I was in college and working full time, I slept about 3 hours a night during the week, with half an hour of sleep during one of my work breaks. On the weekends, I got 8–9 hours of sleep. I did that for years without any adverse effects on my mind or body. Now, I'm comfortable with 5–6 hours of sleep. I choose to eat foods that are healthy and don't require lots of energy to digest (like smoothies), and I believe that helps me need less sleep as well.

If you're not sure the optimal amount of sleep for you, try doing a few 30-day tests on yourself. Sleep for the same amount of time every night for 30 days and see how your body and mind feel. Start with a lesser amount. The less sleep you need, the more time you'll have in life for other things.

> *"Never go to sleep without a request to your subconscious."* –Thomas Edison

Another ritual that you can choose to give yourself is to give your subconscious a task before you go to sleep. This is a good time to review your life goals. It's also a great time for visualization. The subconscious can work on this all night while your physical body is resting. Make sure you have pen and paper by your bed so that you can write any insights that come to you. I've been woken in the middle of the night with insights, and feverishly wrote them down until they stopped, and then went back to bed. This also happens often in the morning when I wake.

Being Okay with the Ebbs and Flows of Life

Sometimes, we are great at sticking to these daily habits. Sometimes, we are not. That's okay. One of the freeing principles is to be okay wherever you are. We are measuring progress, not perfection. Many times, our personal energy is at different levels at different times. I coached a client who had great difficulty with her energy in the wintertime or during extended periods of cloudiness. She was able to combat it a little with lighting and other coping techniques, but in general, her energy was lower during those times of the year. Instead of making herself wrong for feeling like she did (which only brings guilt that doesn't serve), she planned big projects at work and home during those times where her energy level was higher. We are all different, so take advantage of those times when your energy is high, and be gentle on yourself when you need to.

This also needs to be balanced with self-discipline and our inner drive to improve ourselves. It is a fine balance. One thing that I have learned is that action does not come from motivation. Motivation comes from action. If we wait around to do something until we feel motivated, it may never happen. If we choose to act, regardless of how we feel, we soon become motivated. Here's a secret on why this works. When we accomplish something, even a small task, our brain gets a shot of dopamine. Dopamine is a 'feel good' neurotransmitter, so when we begin to act without feeling like it, the dopamine helps provide motivation *after* we have started taking action.

When taking into account the ebbs and flows of life, step back and look at the whole picture, instead of just the current moment. For example, if this was a rough week waking up and getting to the gym for your workout, and you only made it three days this week, instead of all five, figure out why it happened. Were you working later, so you got to bed later? How were you eating? What other factors may have contributed to this? Don't look for excuses, look for reasons. Also, look at a broader time period. Sure this week was rough, but is your trend for the past 3-6 months progressing or regressing? Are you becoming more balanced in all your daily habits?

Each habit is a brick in your personal investment building. One brick doesn't make a building, nor does one habit make a balanced life. As you take all of your personal daily investments into consideration, you can determine the amount of progress you are truly making in improving yourself.

THE FINAL CHAPTER
IS ONLY THE BEGINNING

*N*OW THAT WE'VE BEEN THROUGH the content of Zenpowerment in this book, I'd like to share my Zenpowerment Credo again, to see if it makes more sense to you now, than it did at the beginning of this book:

Zenpowerment Credo

1. There are two primary motivational forces in our lives; love and fear. Love unites, fear divides. Love accepts, fear resists. Love is proactive, fear is reactive. Love is intrinsic, fear is learned. With love, there must be a balance between love for ourselves and love for others. This balance is created by boundaries. **I choose love.**

2. I give away my power when I come from fear or choose to react from programming. **I choose to stand in my power.**

3. I am responsible for all that is in my life. I have the power to choose my response and to give meaning to all circumstances. **I choose to stand in my power.**

4. I cannot change the past. It has been a great teacher, and I honor it. My future is not guaranteed, but I can establish a direction for my future. The only thing that really exists is here and now. It is the only place of action. **I choose to live intentionally in the present.**

5. My authenticity has been covered by years of filters and programming, through family, education, corporations, culture, government, tradition, authority, and many other things. Filters and programming include attachment, judgments, labels, expectations, comparison, emotions, and our experiences. I empty my cup of knowledge to see what still serves and what does not. I choose to always keep the principles of love, trust, respect, communication, service, gratitude, and fun in my cup. **I choose to uncover my authenticity.**

6. I believe that attachment to opinions, knowledge, people, things, expectations, outcomes, thoughts, emotions, the past and future causes great suffering. **I choose non-attachment.**

7. I believe that saying no to the many unessential things allows me greater time and energy to focus on those things I deem important. By doing this, I become more efficient. **I choose to live essentially.**

8. I have believed that I am a separate, independent being. I now believe that we are all interconnected beings, all made up of energy. **I choose love for all living things.**

9. Every act and habit empowers or disempowers me, and continues to build up over time. I am a sum of my thoughts, words, actions, and habits. **I choose empowering habits.**

10. **I choose empowerment by living intentionally and authentically.**

See if these resonate more with you now than they did at the beginning. As you integrate these principles into your life, I challenge you to write your own credo and review it on a daily basis. It will change you.

Now that you've finished this book, the journey has only just begun. I've been learning and practicing these principles for the past 18 years, and I still have so much to learn and deeper to go in my internal journey. I have not shared everything I've learned in this book, only the beginning parts to get you started. If I were to share as much as I've learned to date, you'd think for sure that I was a crackpot, just like when the Wright brothers wanted to fly. It's possible, but as Lao Tzu said, the journey of a thousand miles begins with a single step. If you embrace these principles and apply them in your life, this is the first step.

Thank you for taking this journey with me. I wish you success in your travels. If you wish to continue on this journey with me, you may connect with me at my website, myzenpowerment.com, or on Facebook at facebook.com/zenpowerment.

If you're interested in meeting with me and a group of really cool people for weekly coaching on Zenpowerment, join me at the Closet Hippie Club (joinus.closethippie.club).

ABOUT THE AUTHOR

RANDALL H. SCOTT is an author, speaker, coach, and the founder of Zenpowerment. With a degree in marketing, Randy spent a 25-year corporate career in international sales and marketing, while living in the U.S., Europe and Asia.

After nearly dying in a motorcycle accident at the age of 33, he realized that he had a second chance to live, so went in search of what really matters in life. His passion for the fusion of science and spirituality led him to compile the principles and tools of Zenpowerment. He's found a way to enjoy more peace, power and purpose in life, as well as discover authenticity by uncovering who we are not in order to find out who we really are.

Made in the USA
San Bernardino, CA
20 March 2018